Padi Kolam

An artistic tradition

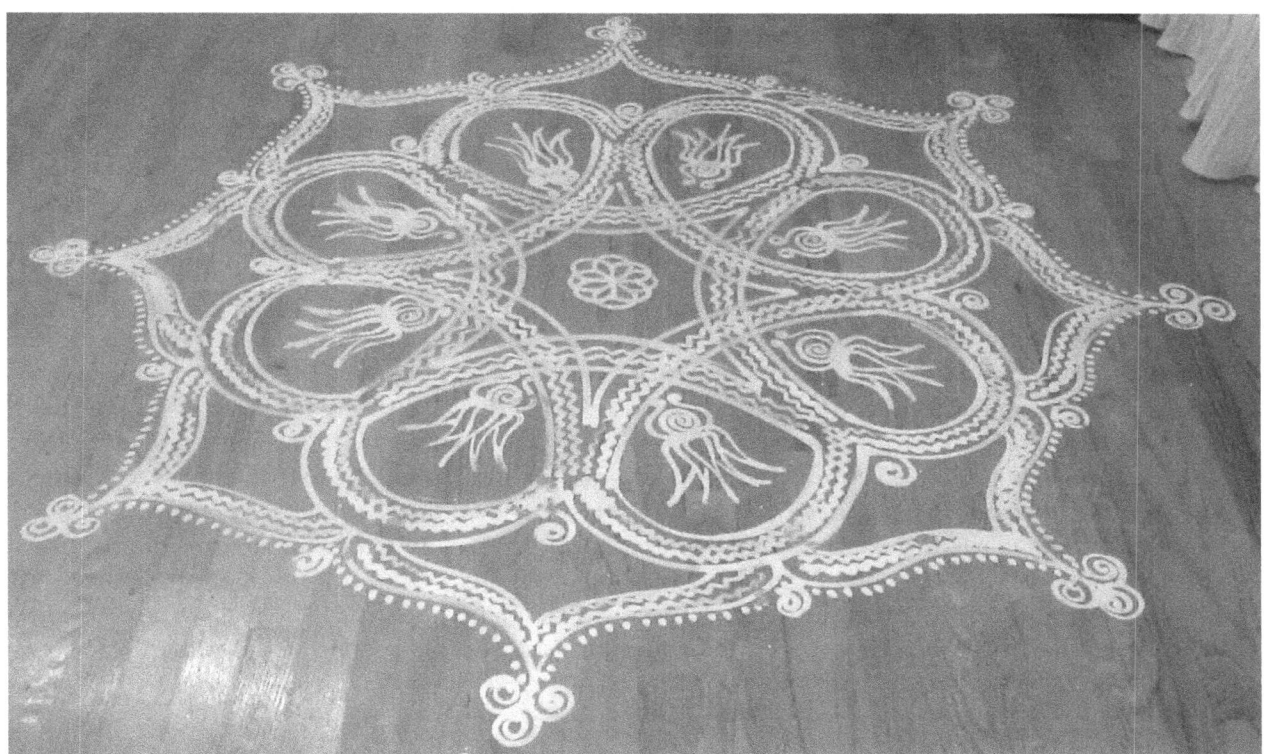

Edition I
Vikram

Preface

There is an artistic tradition of decorating the floor with beautiful floral patterns. In north India it is called Rangoli and in Tamil Nadu it is called Kolam. There are some variants of the Kolam. One variant involves making neat patterns on a grid made of dots. Another variant involves snaking patterns made of plaited lines passing around a dot grid. Padi Kolam is another variant of the Kolam. It is very rich and harder than the other forms. Artists make exquisite symmetric patterns with bare hands. No engineering tools, no dot grids and not even a ruler. In addition, they are drawn impromptu! Yet the Kolams are spectacular. These Kolams lend a sense of beauty and grace to occasions like marriages, family functions and festivals. It also expresses the mood of a house. The more expansive the Kolam in front of a house, the happier they are. This book also contains a small collection of non Padi Kolams by Janbagalakshmi, Mala and many other unknown artists from Chennai and Kumbakonam regions.

The Padi Kolam style is predominantly a tradition of Tamil Brahmins. There is no book definition of a Padi Kolam. It does have some key differentiating features – a concave square or a straight square made of multiple parallel lines at the center with floral decorations at its corners. The central concave square or straight square feature is called the "Padi". There is also rotational symmetry. If any Padi Kolam is rotated by 90 degrees it will still be identical. Some of them have finer rotational symmetries of 30 degrees and 45 degrees. The lines forming the Kolam are drawn in three ways. The most common one is by applying coarse rice flour on the floor with bare hands. The practice of using Rice flour is to show compassion for other creatures, like, insects, birds and animals that feed on it. Sometimes the rice flour is mixed with white rock powder called Kolamavu, literally meaning Kolam powder. The second one called the Ezhai Kolam is drawn using a paste made from rice flour and water. As it dries, the Kolam appears in a magnificent bright white color. Yet another method of drawing the lines is using a drum filled with powder. The drum has holes through which some powder can come out. As the drum is rolled on the floor, beautiful lines with inlaid patterns are created on the floor. Flowers are the most typical inlaid patterns found in these roller drums. It is worth noting that the Padi should be drawn with a minimum of two lines. Single line Padi is considered inauspicious. Sometimes, for auspicious occasions, thick red (Kaavi) lines are drawn adjacent to the Padi. This gives the Kolam a nice contrast. It can be seen in some of the Kolams in this collection.

The origin of the Padi Kolam is not known to me either. There is at least one reference from the poet Andal about Kolams in general. In one of her works, she pleads with her favorite god Krishna to not spoil her Kolam that she made with back breaking labor. Possibly this tradition can be traced back to prehistoric times!

This wonderful tradition is in decline. With modernization there is less time and space to learn or practice this art. The younger generation is learning it lesser and lesser. Pretty soon there will be only very few artists who can do this in its traditional splendor. This book is about preserving this art for posterity and encouraging the readers to collect photographs of these Kolams and also learn and practice it. I acknowledge that these Kolams were photographed on different occasions and I have not drawn them myself. Some were obtained from albums of friends and relatives. Wherever known, I have mentioned the author name. Camera technology was not that great in mobile phones some years back. The Kolams look much more magnificent when seen in person, in broad daylight. Across the thousands of villages and towns in Tamil Nadu, many beautiful Kolams are being drawn on a daily basis. To give an idea of the magnificence of these Kolams and to avoid the perspective distortion caused by a camera, I have included a computer redrawing of the first Kolam. Perspective distortion is what happens when one takes a picture of two parallel lines. Instead of being parallel, they appear to slant towards each other and meet at some point. The computer redrawing was done using the free and open source software Inkscape. I would love to redraw all of them. May be, the readers can help me with this! In the current times, these patterns may be given a new and different life in garments, carpets, floor tiles and architectural features. As drawing a Kolam involves a lot of hard work it can be seen as Art Yoga that keeps the body fit and the mind creative!

Thrivikraman Murali
3vikram.murali@gmail.com
April 2014

Dedicated to the masters of Padi Kolams and all artists in general.

Contents

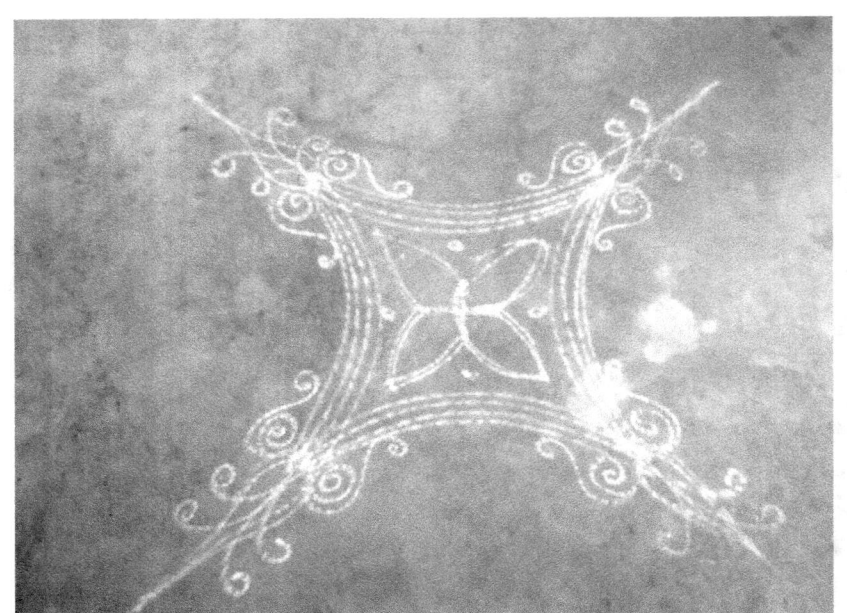

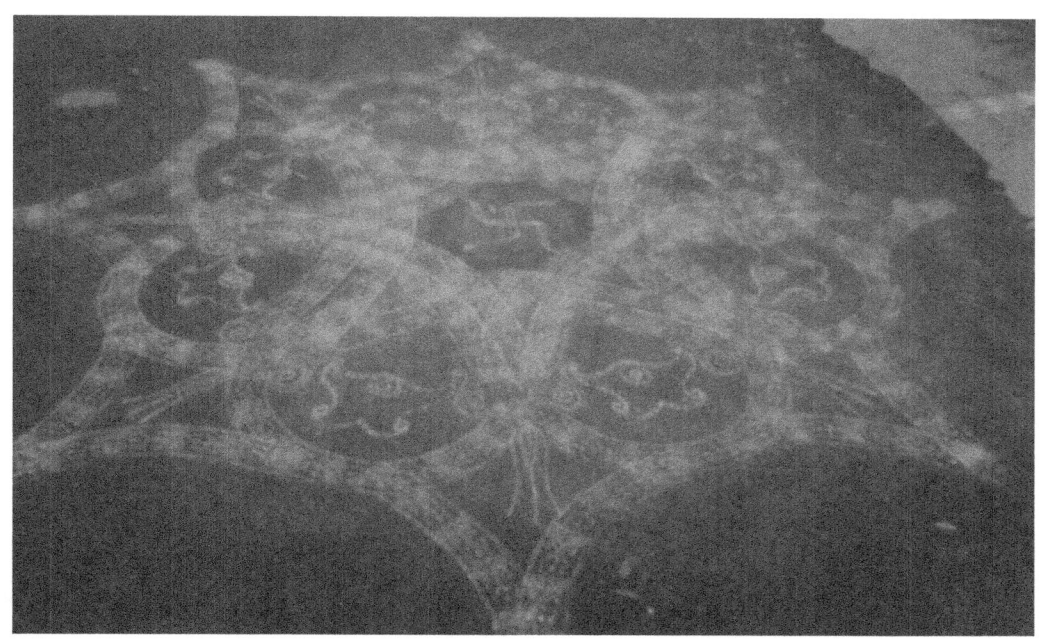

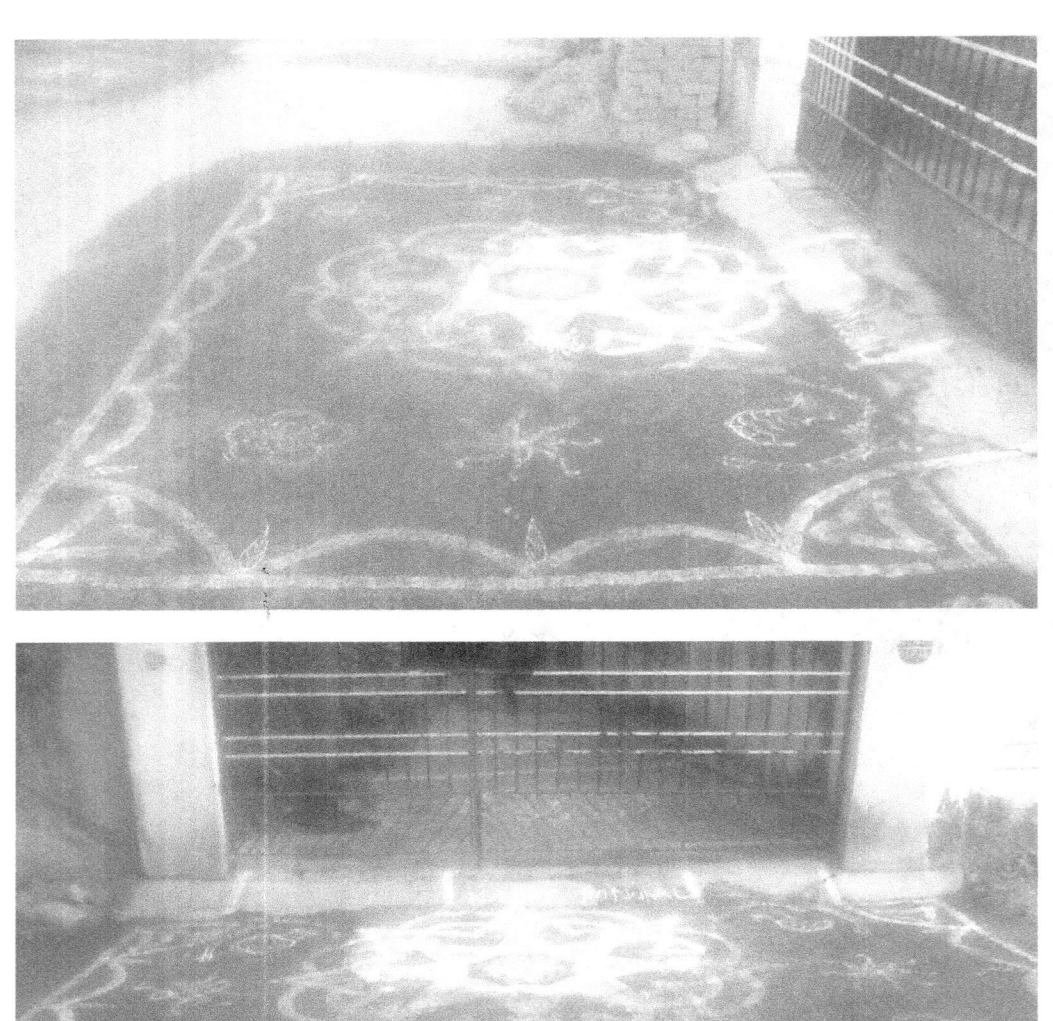

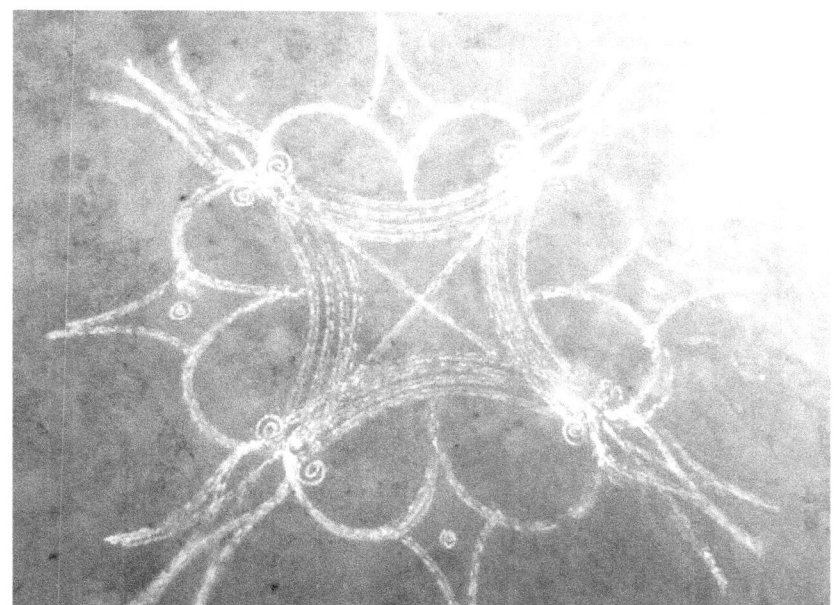

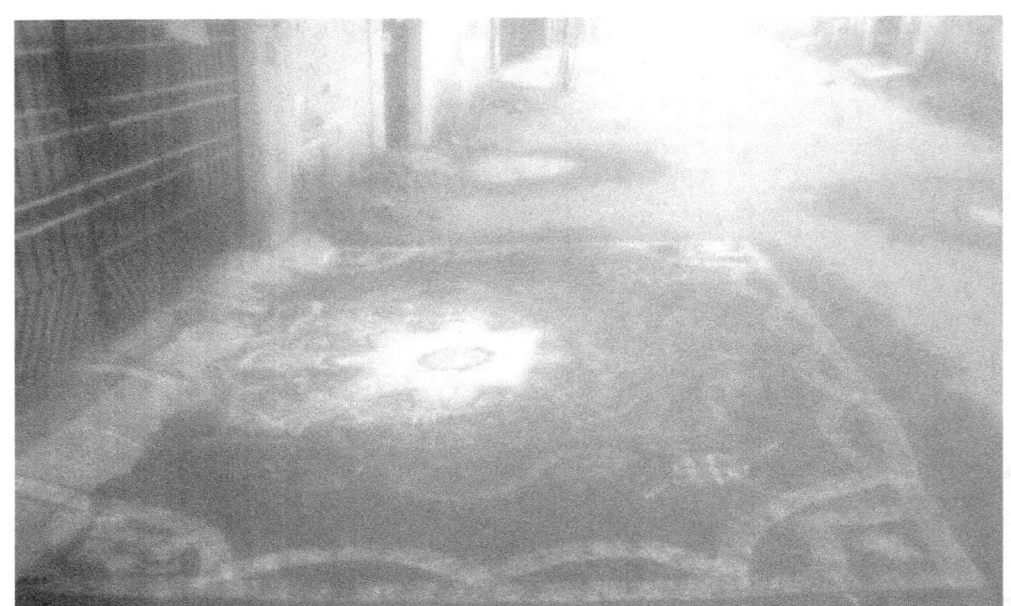

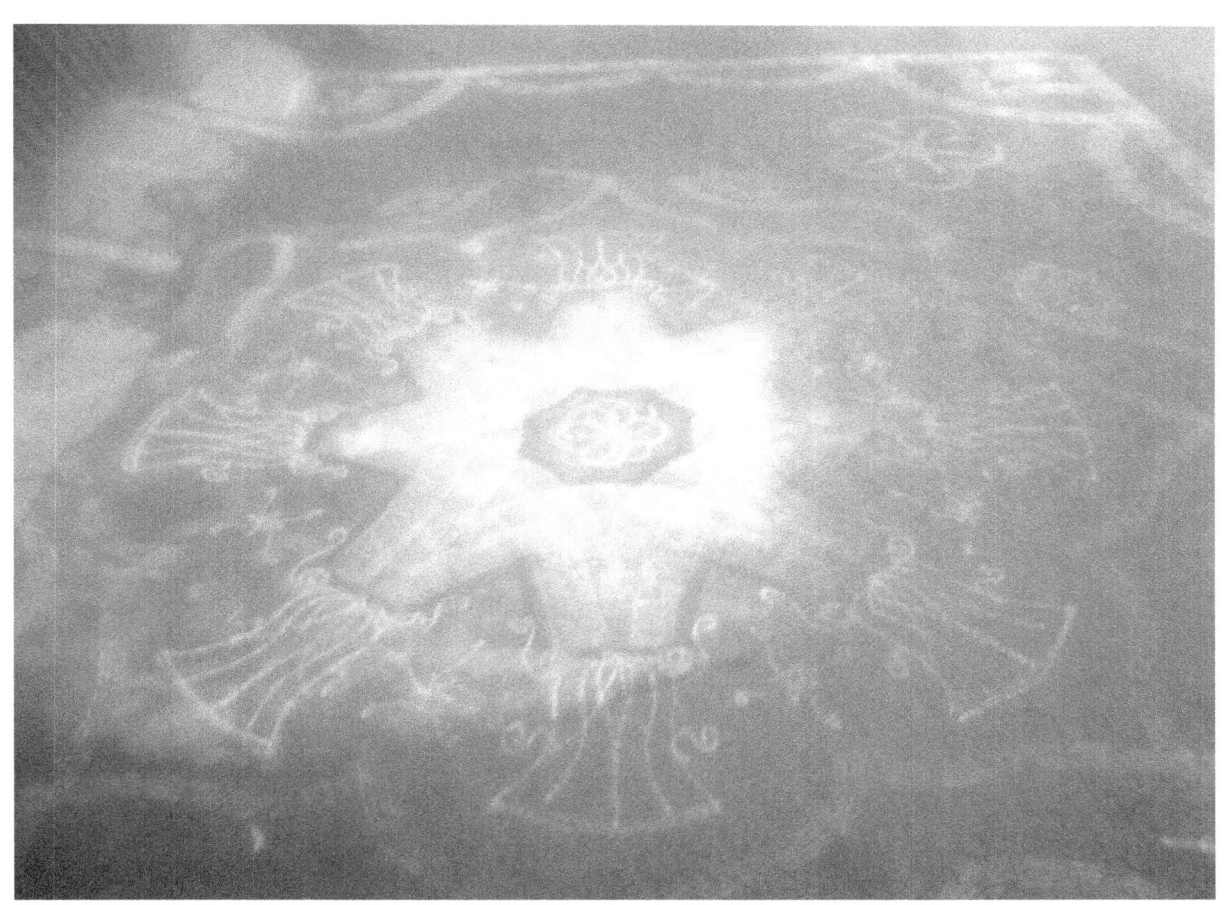

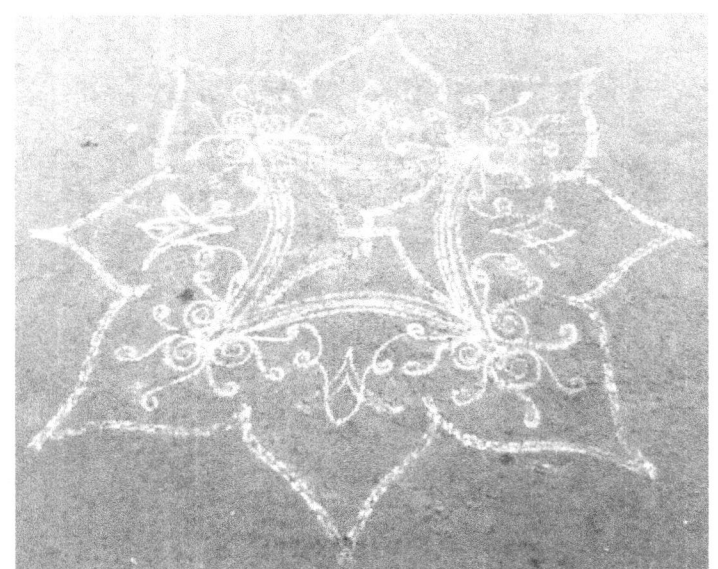

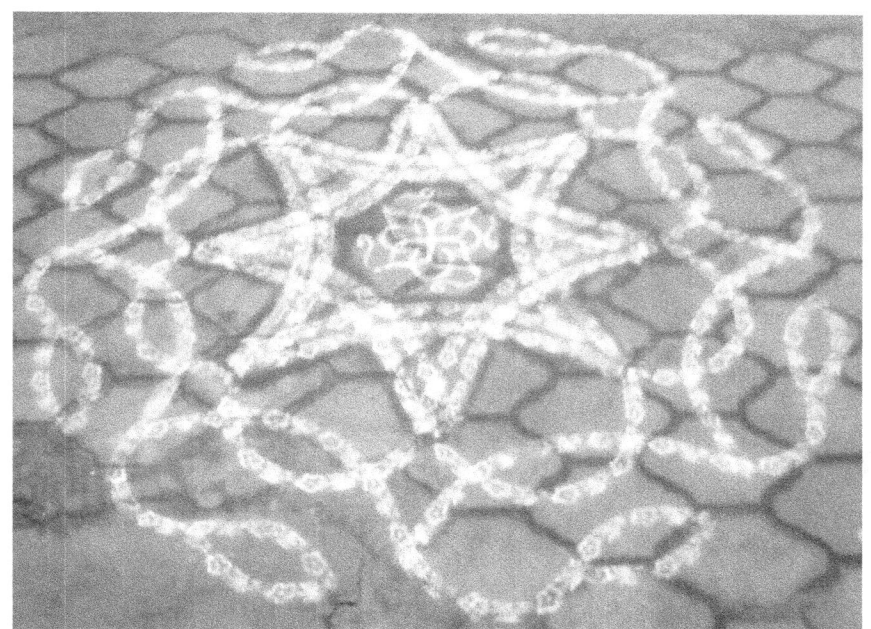

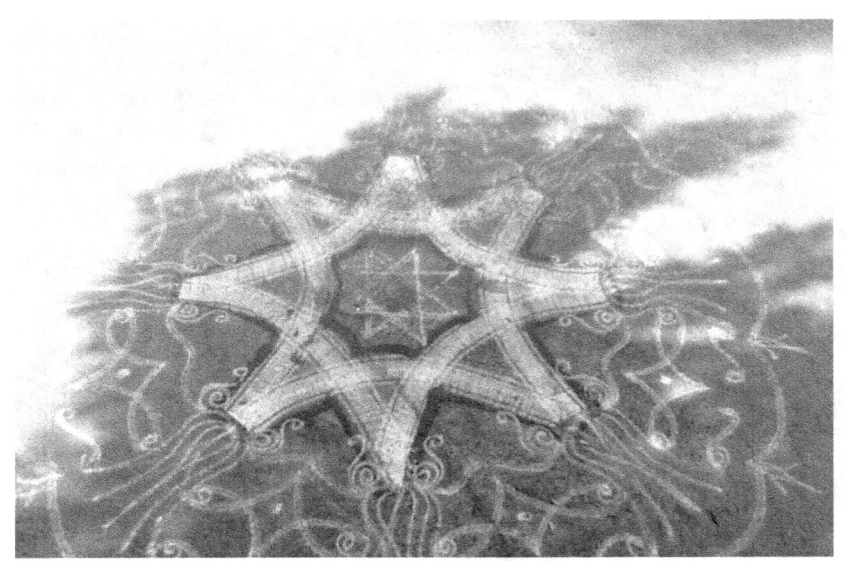

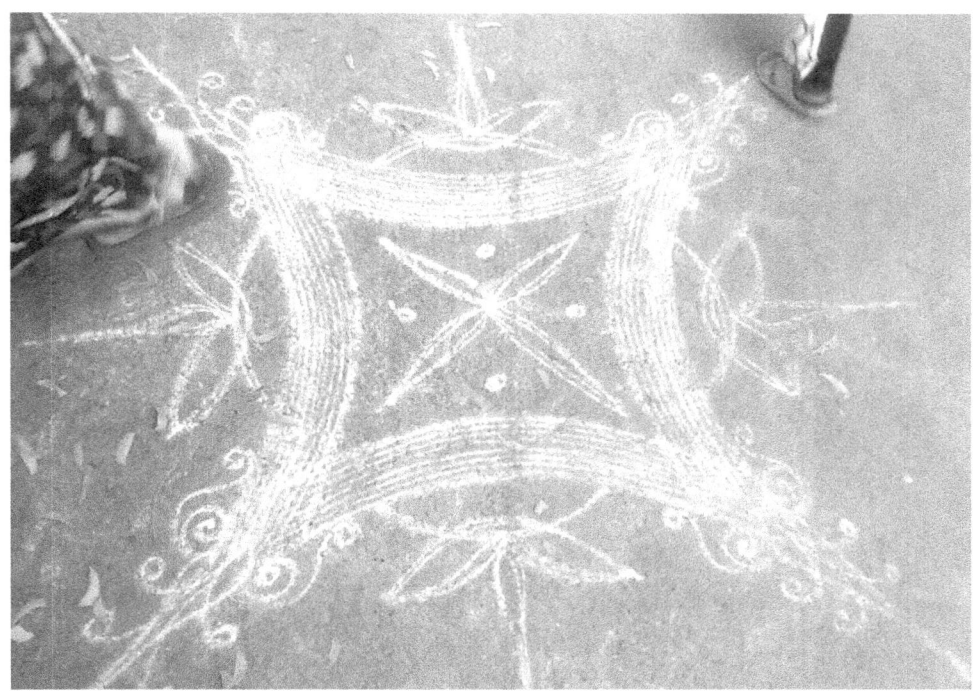

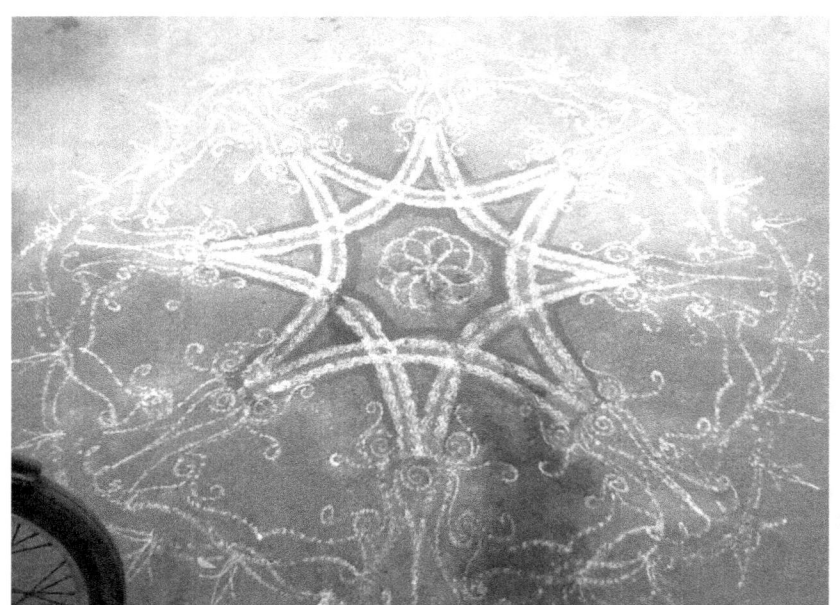

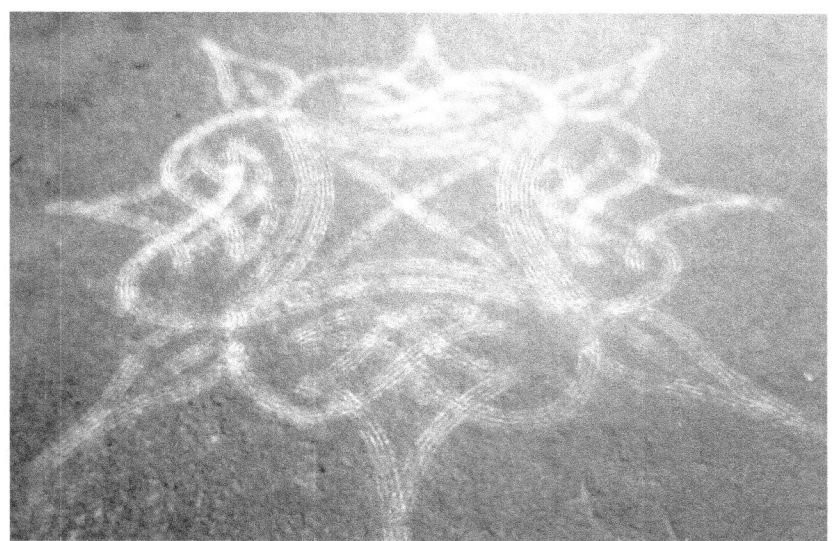

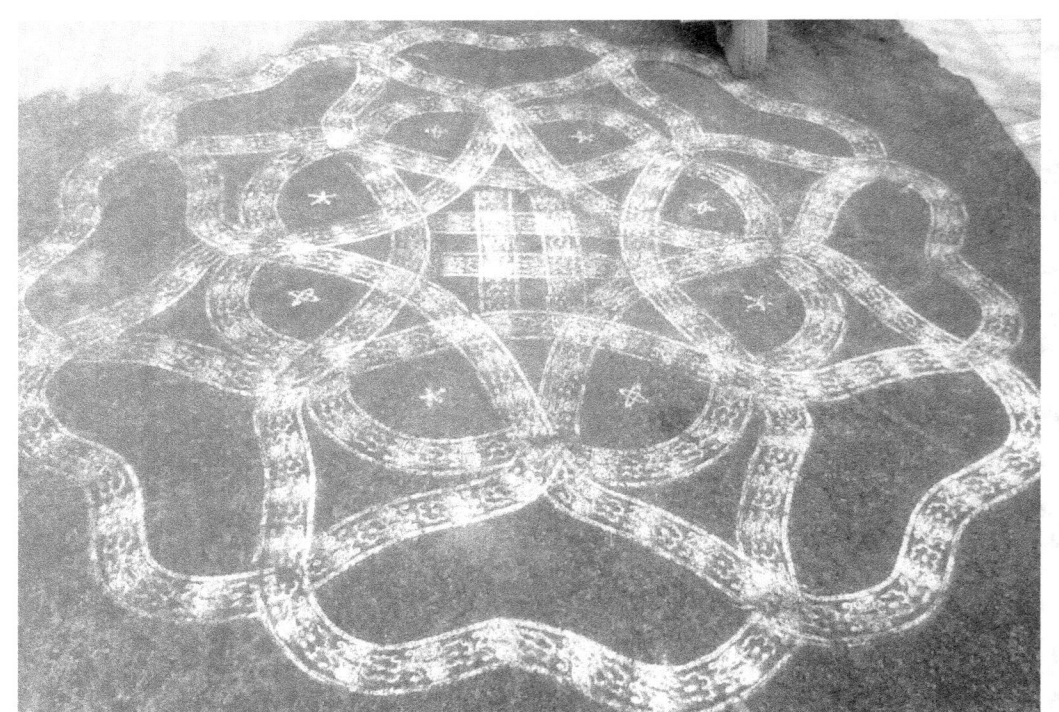

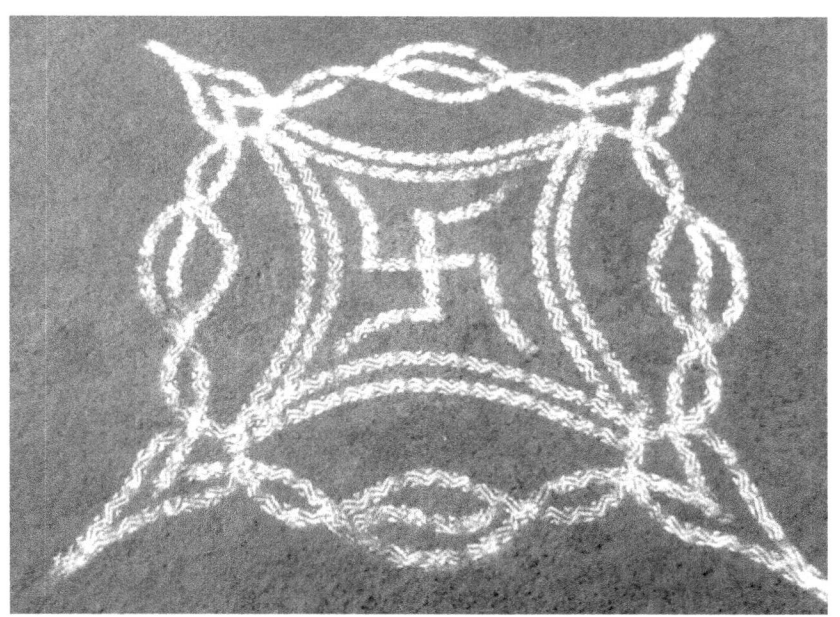

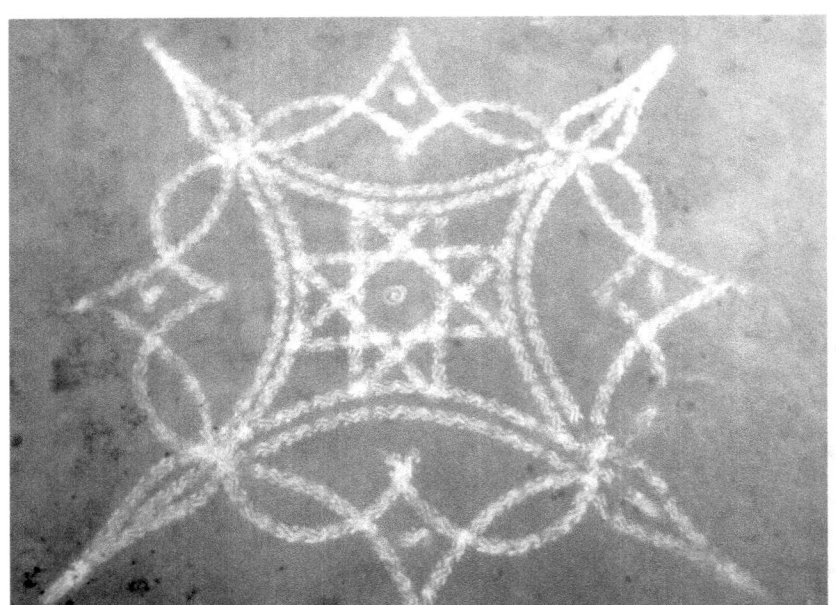

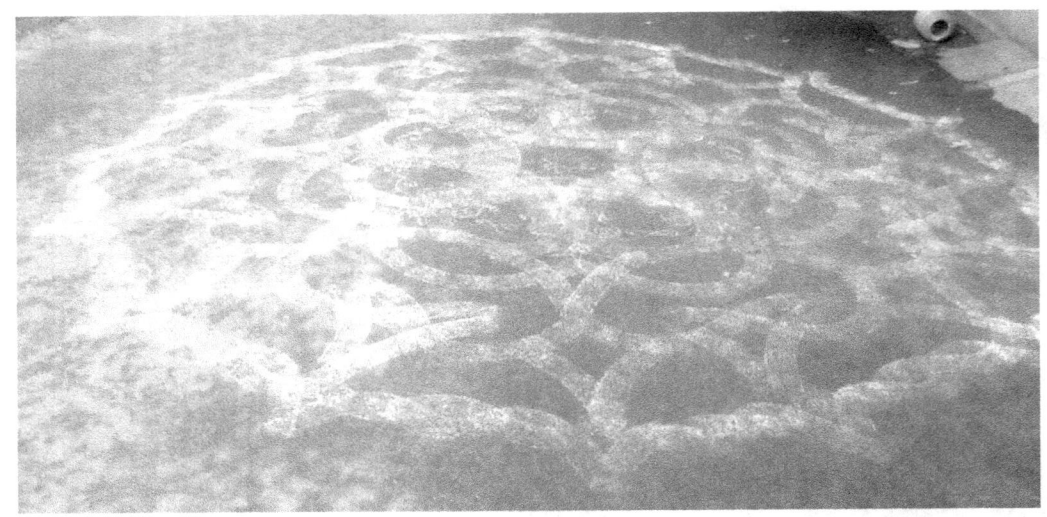

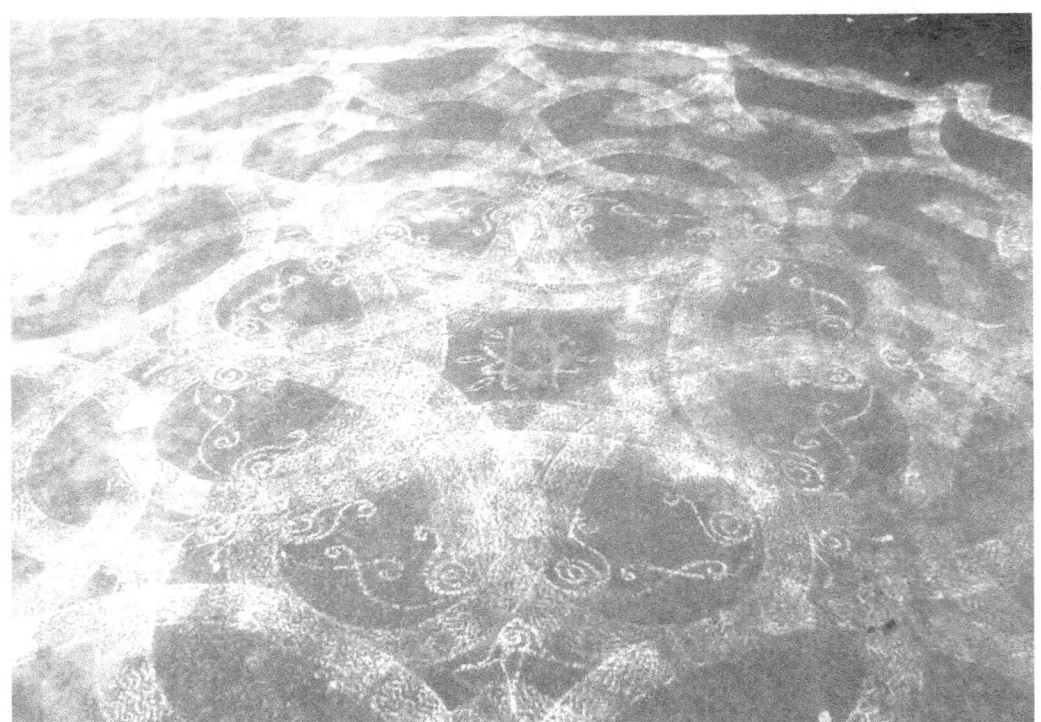

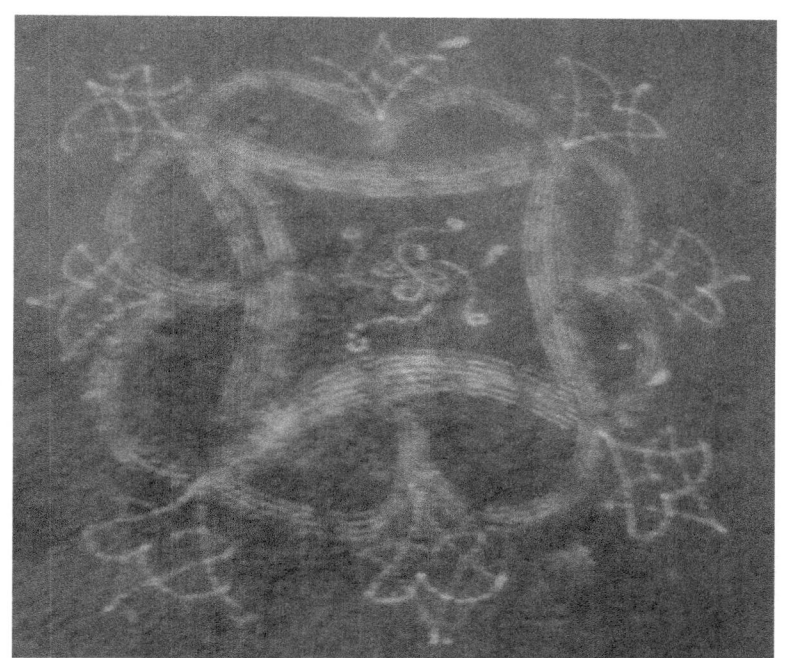

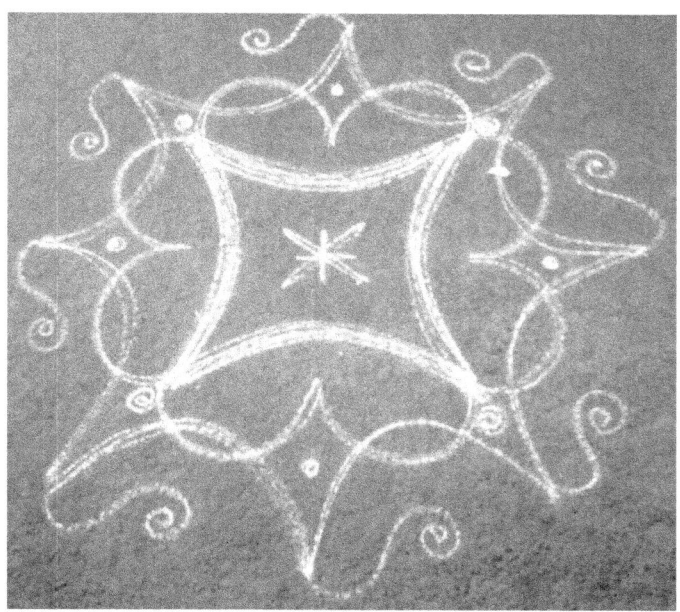

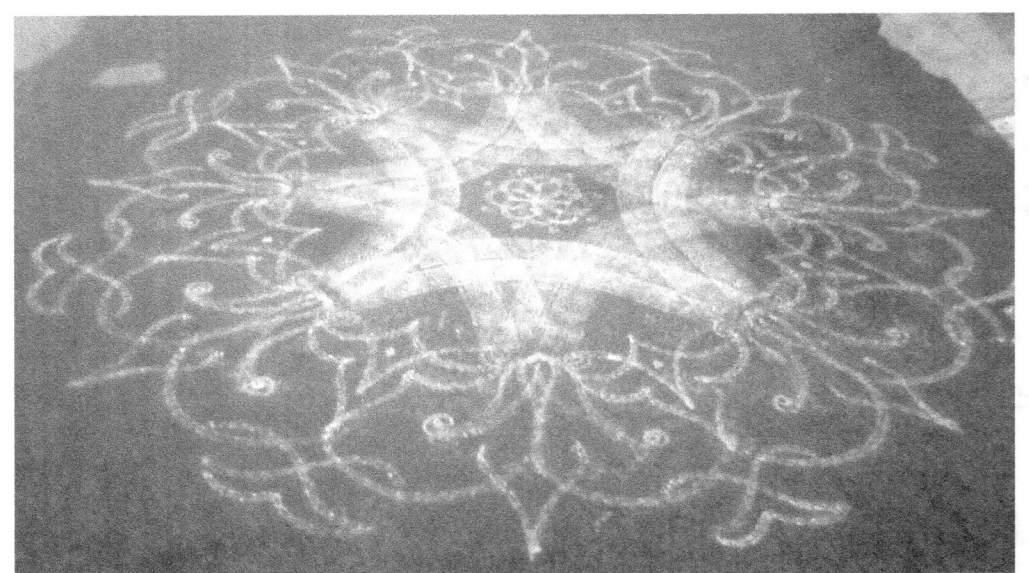

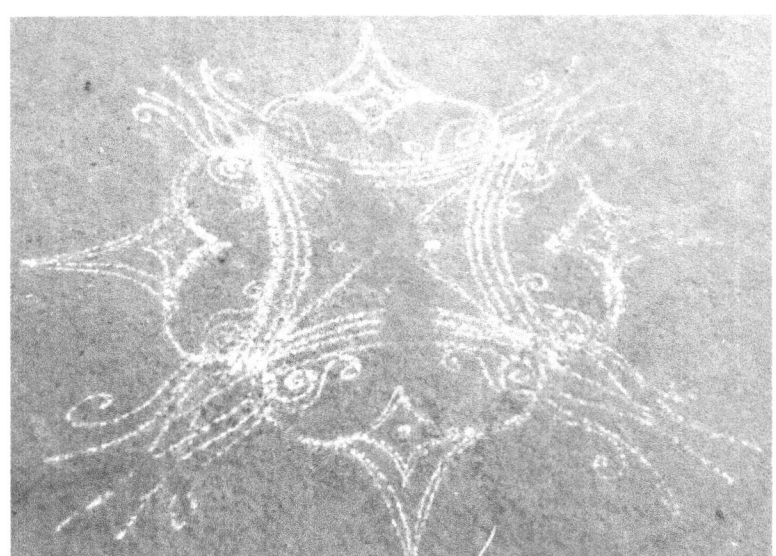

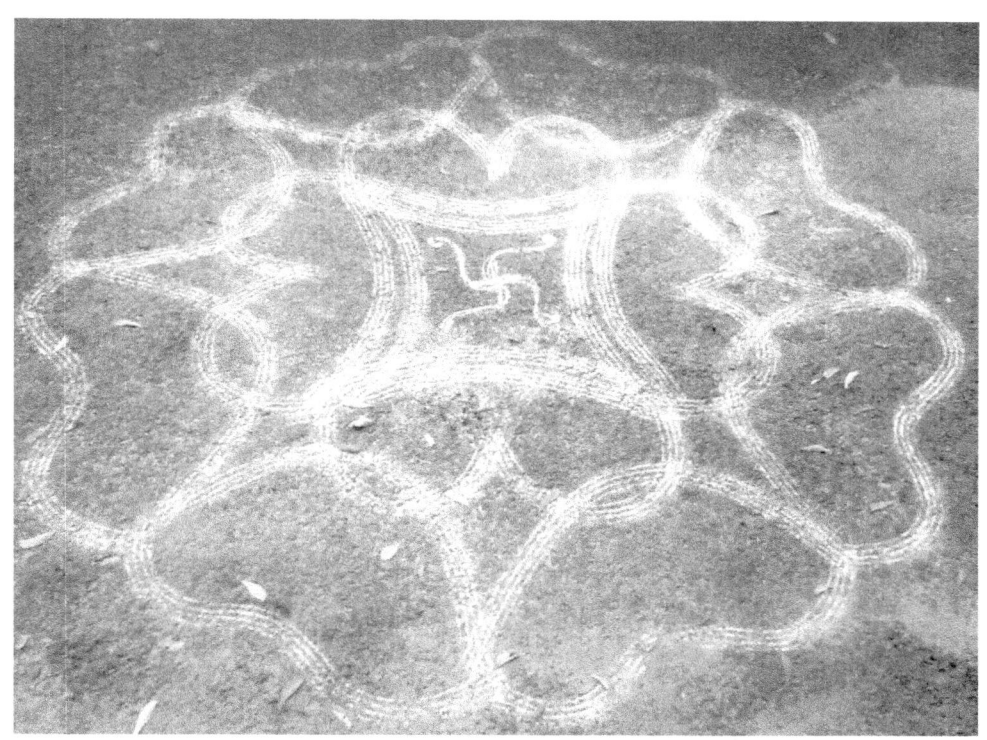

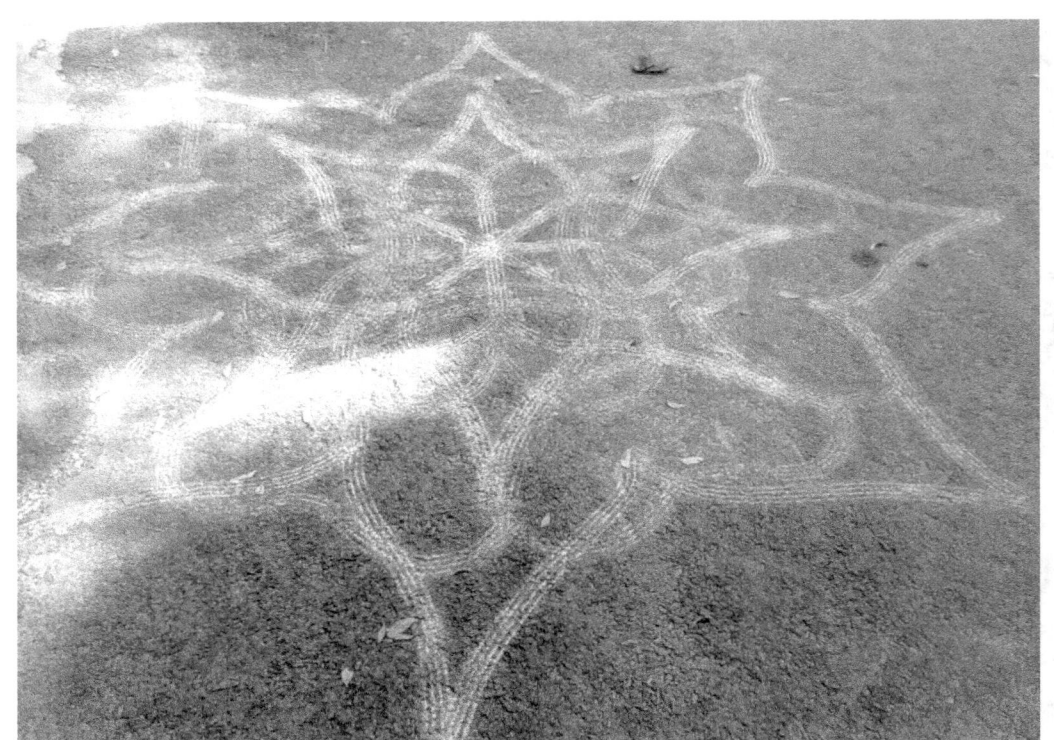

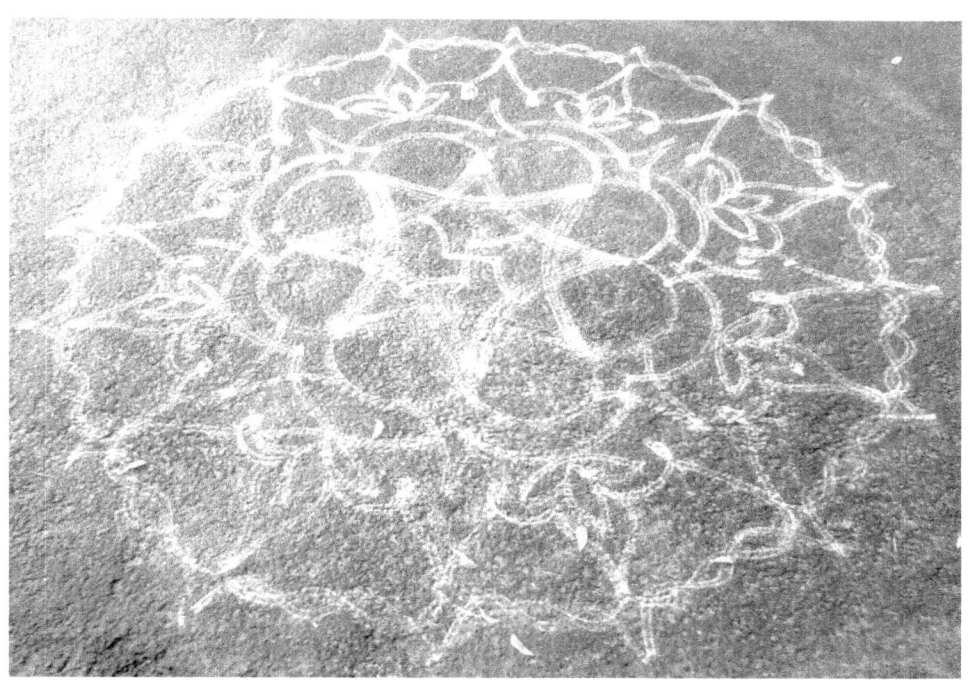

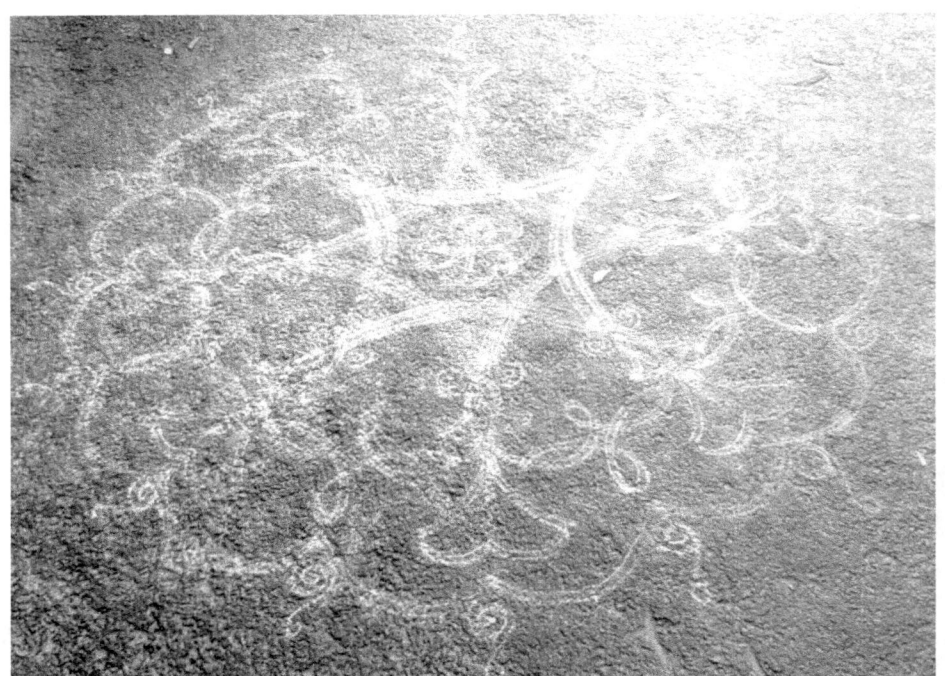

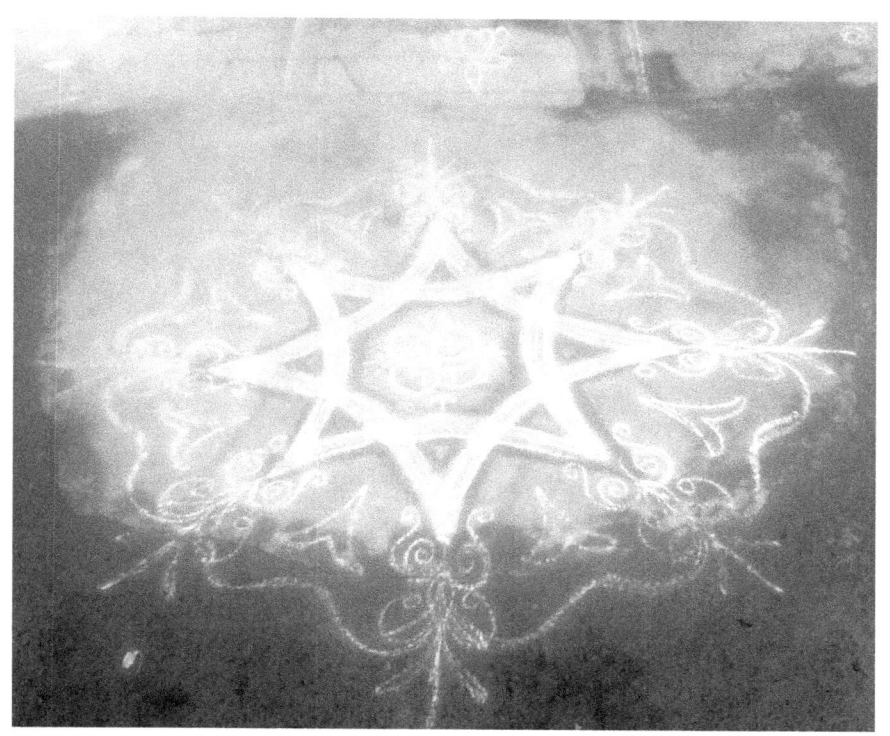

Mala's kolams

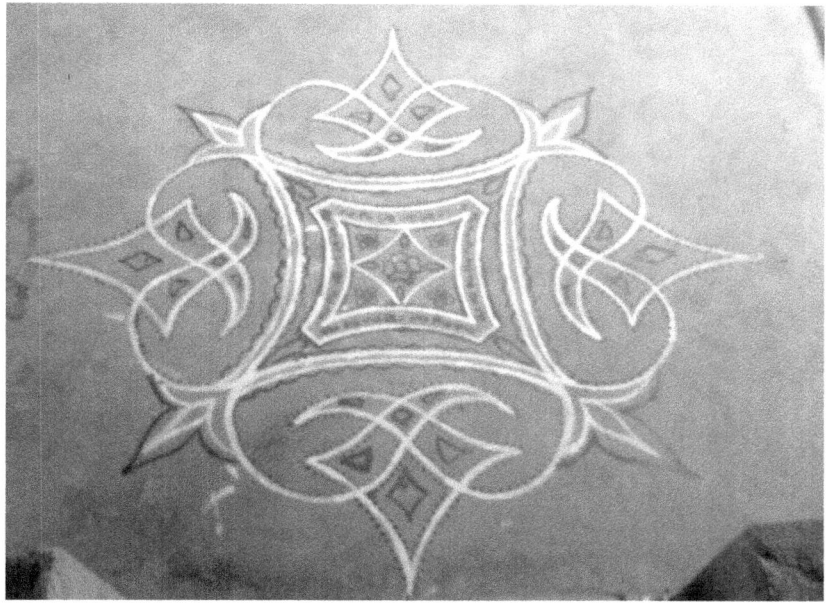

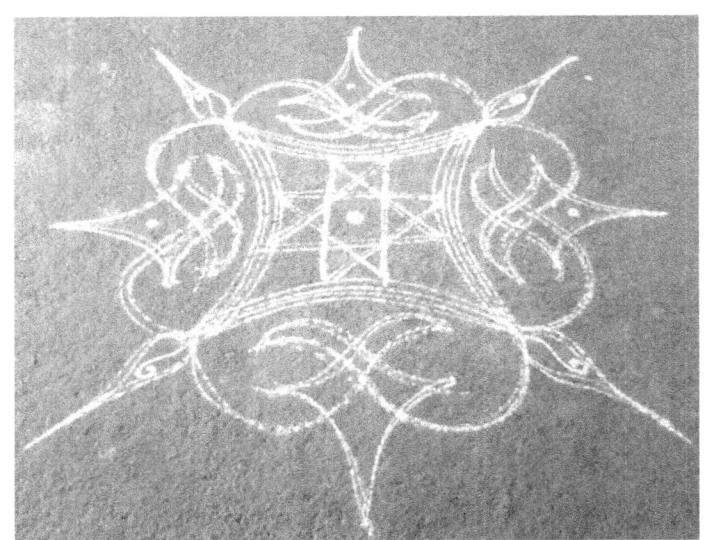

Jayalakshmi's Kolams

Prabhavati's Kolams

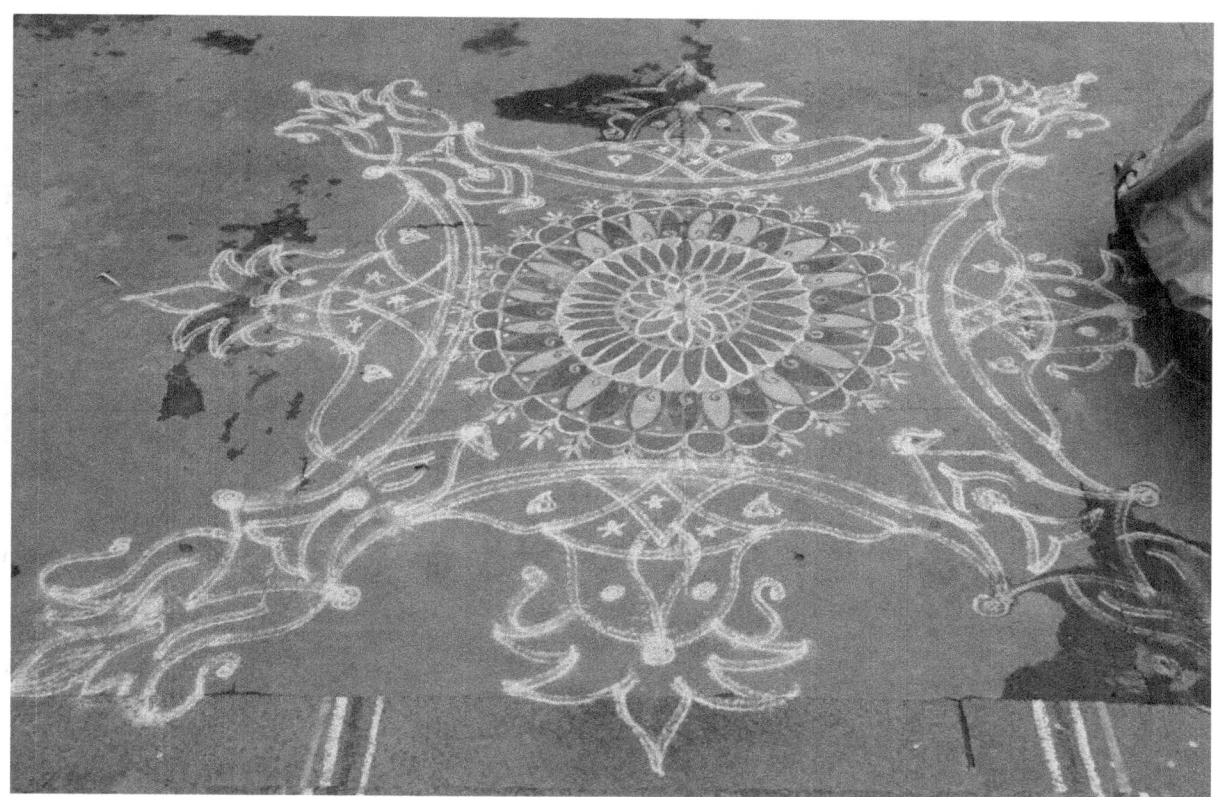

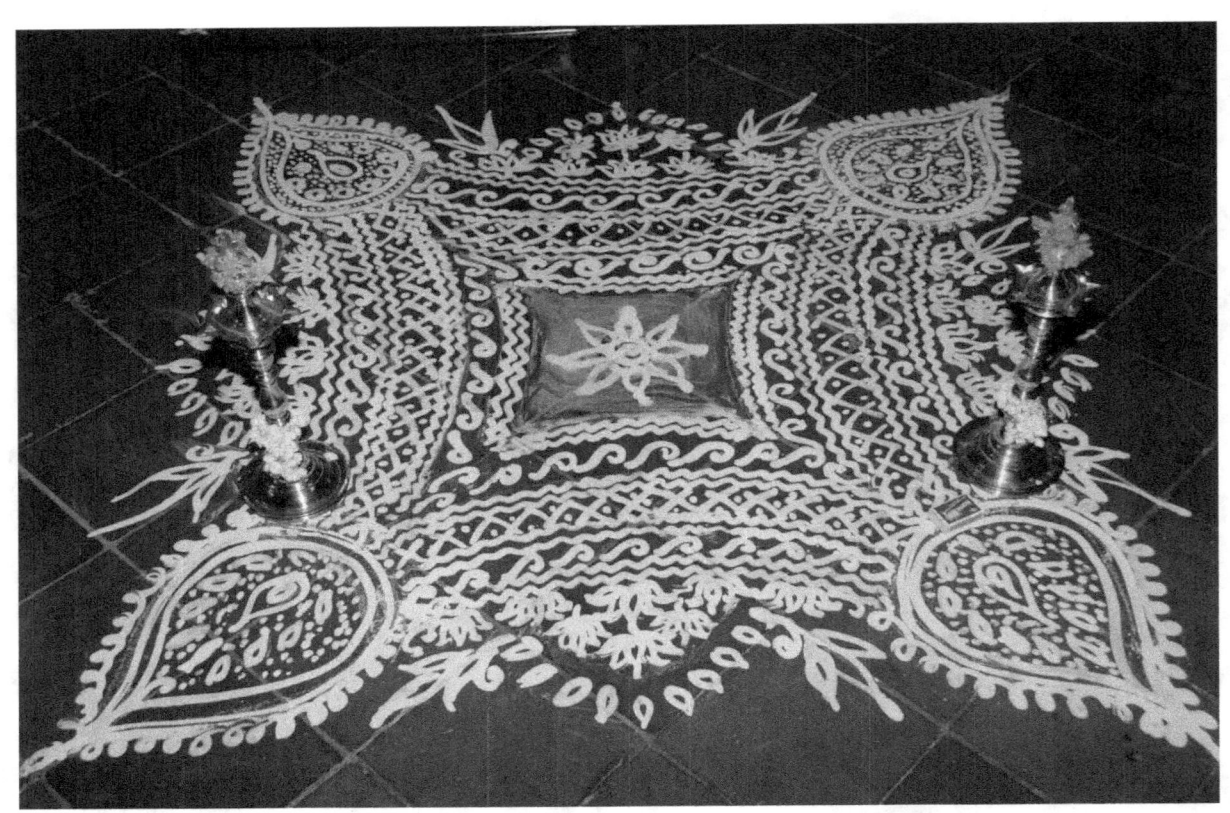

Nachiar's Kolams

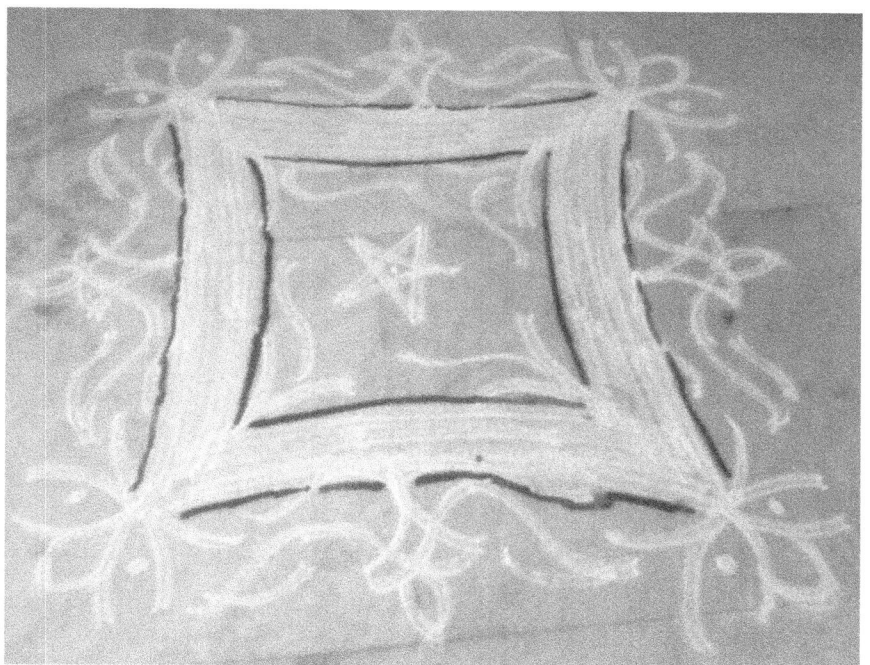

Aravinda's Kolam

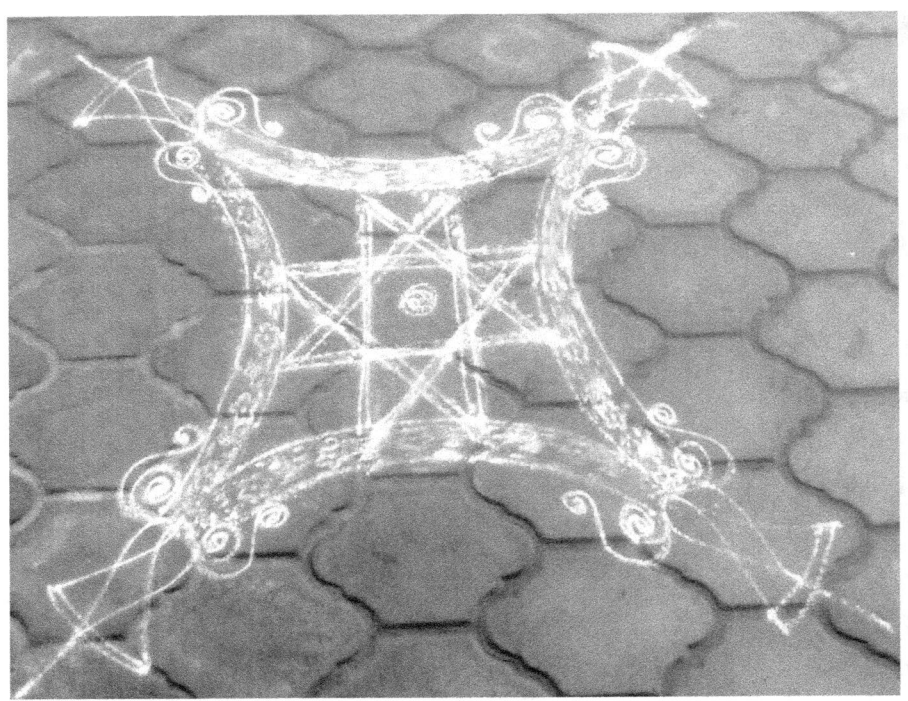

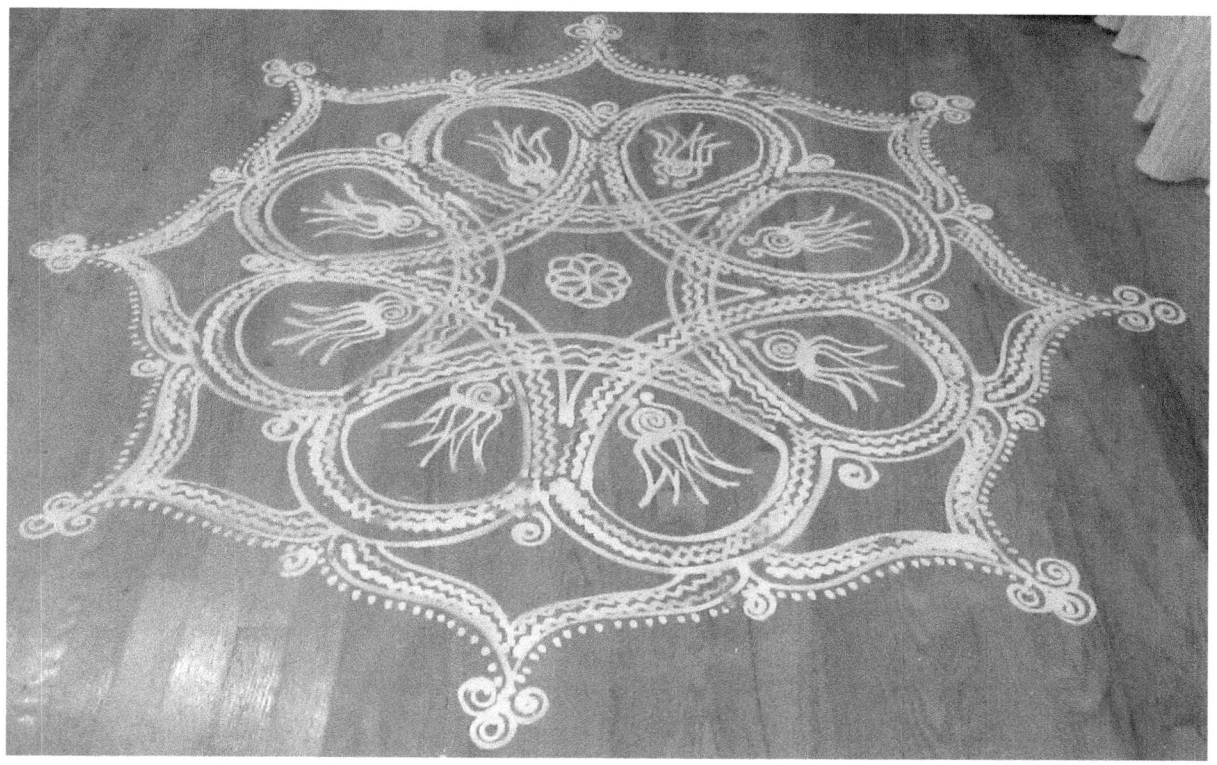

Sudha's Kolams

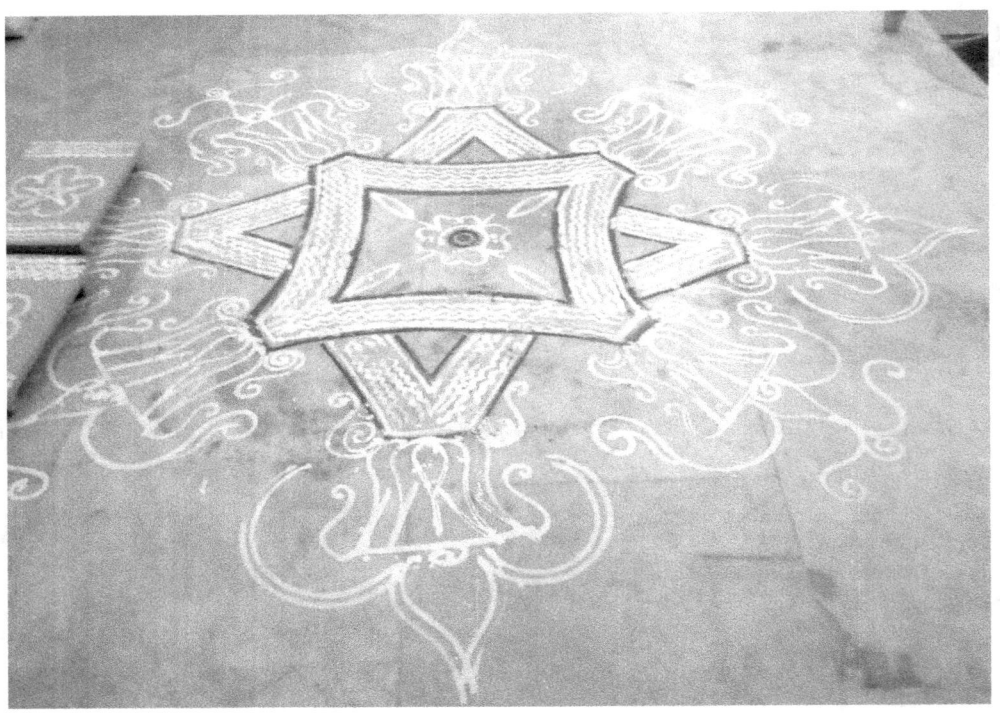

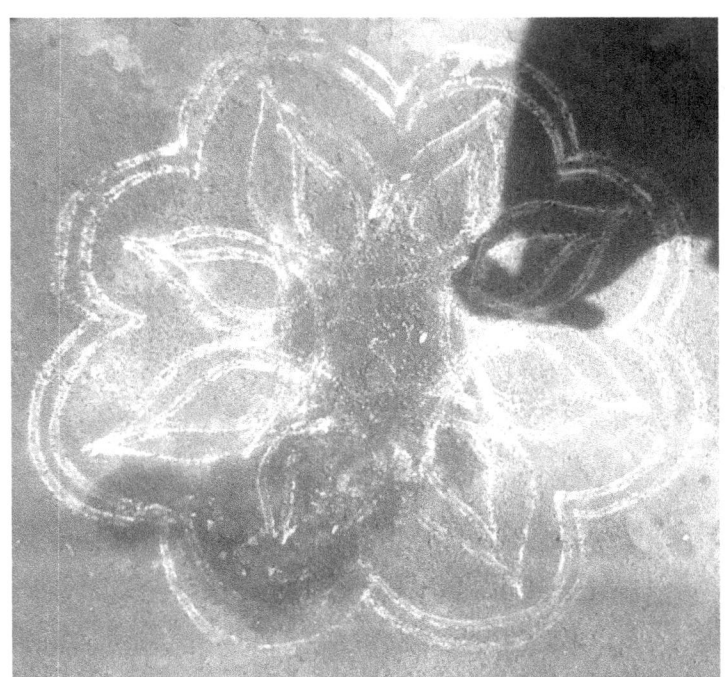

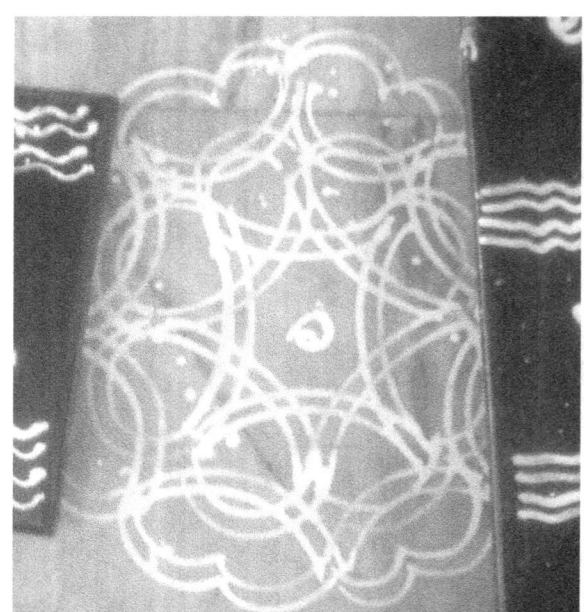

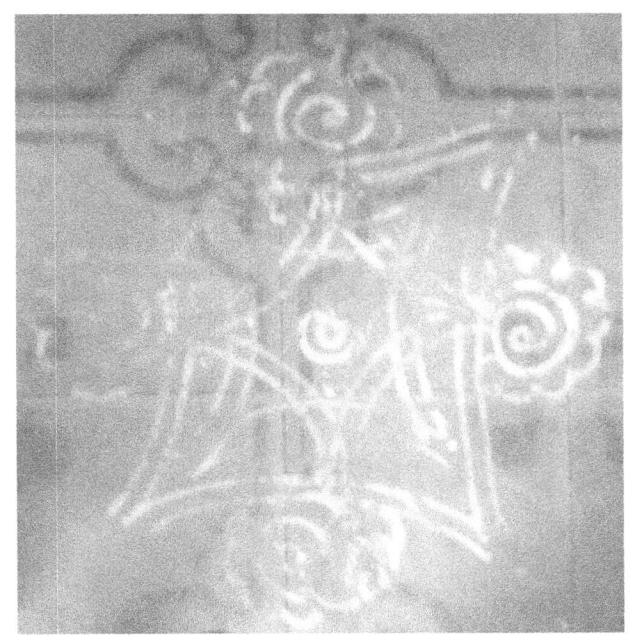

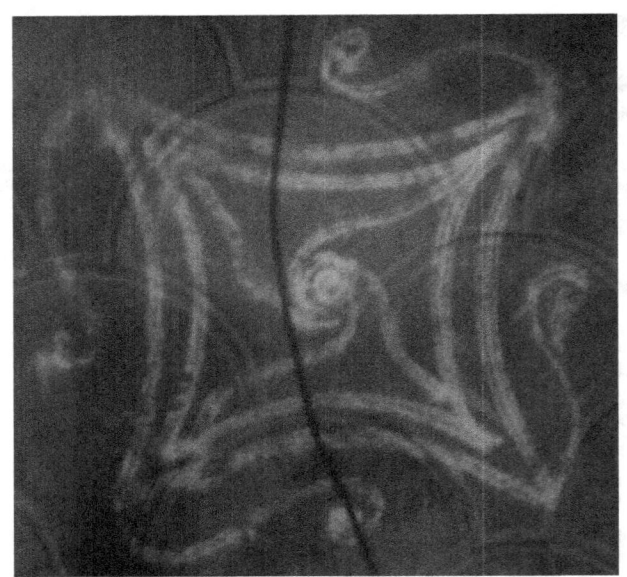

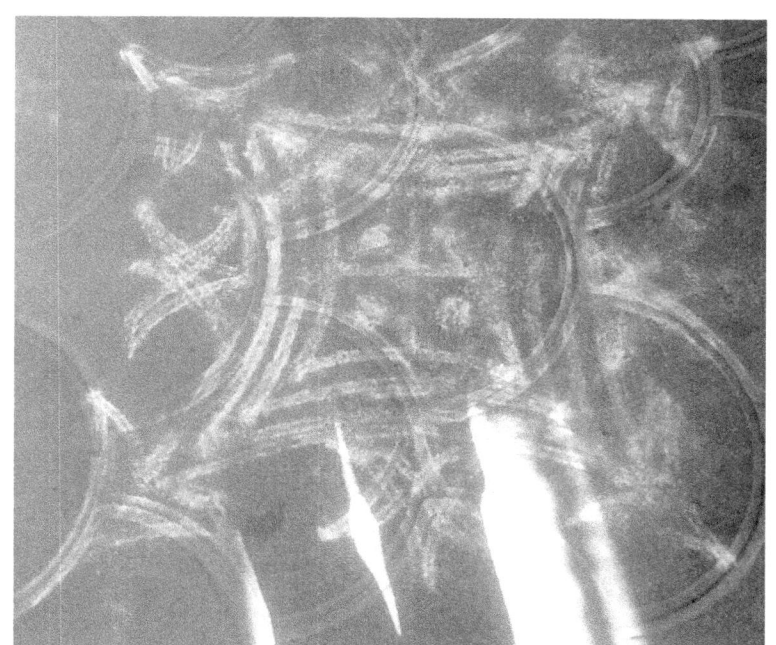

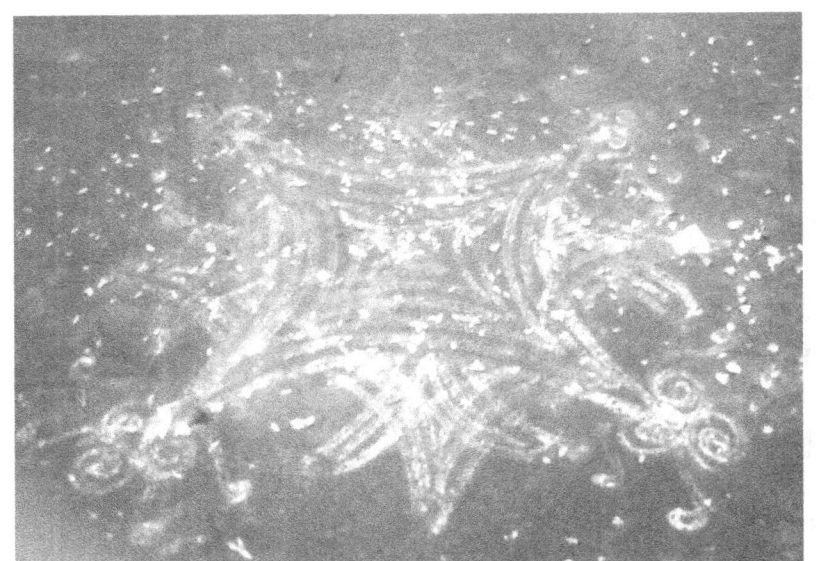

Kolams from unknown artists from Srirangam

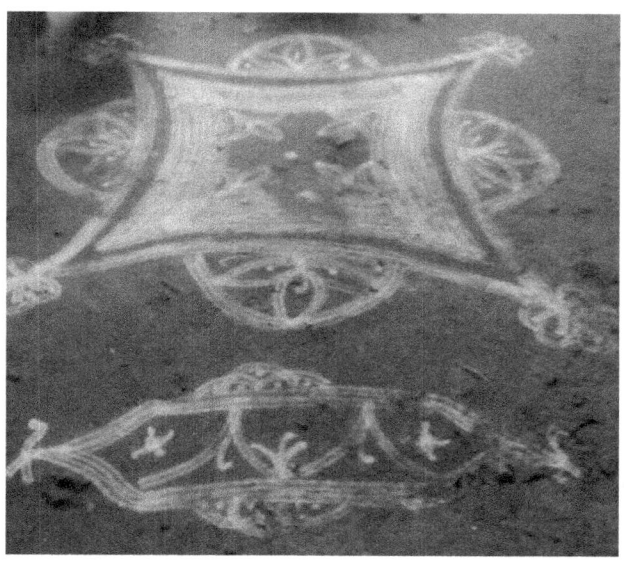

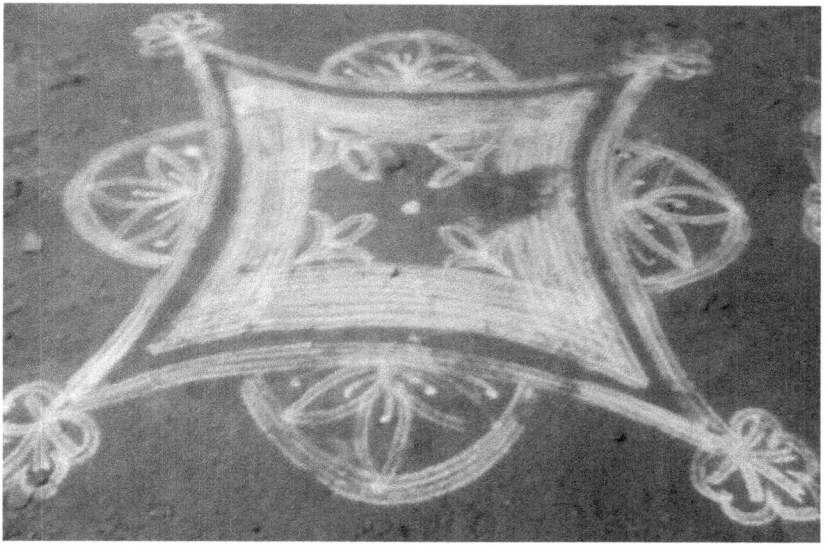

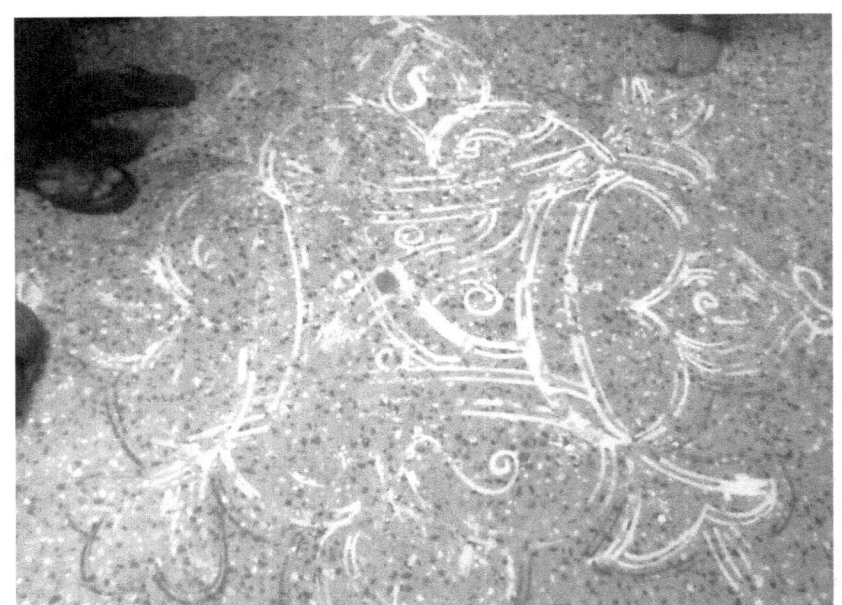

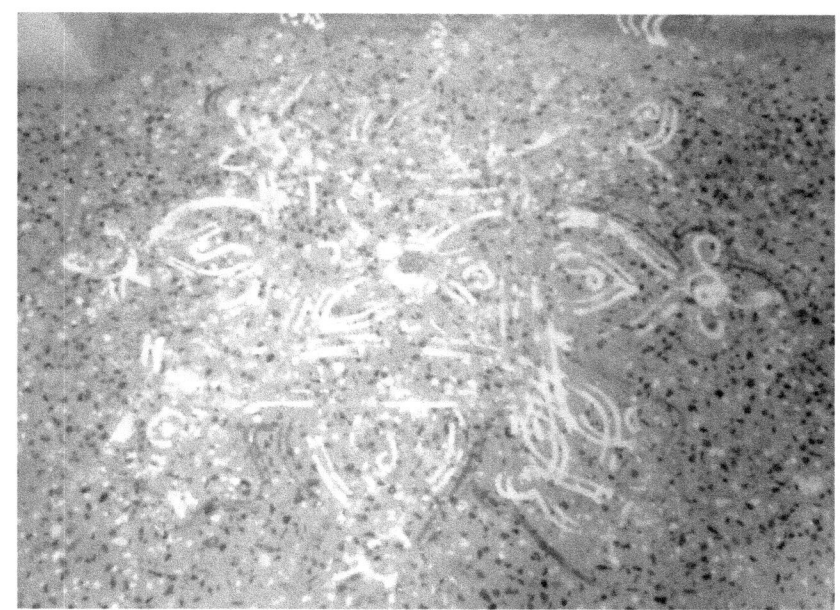

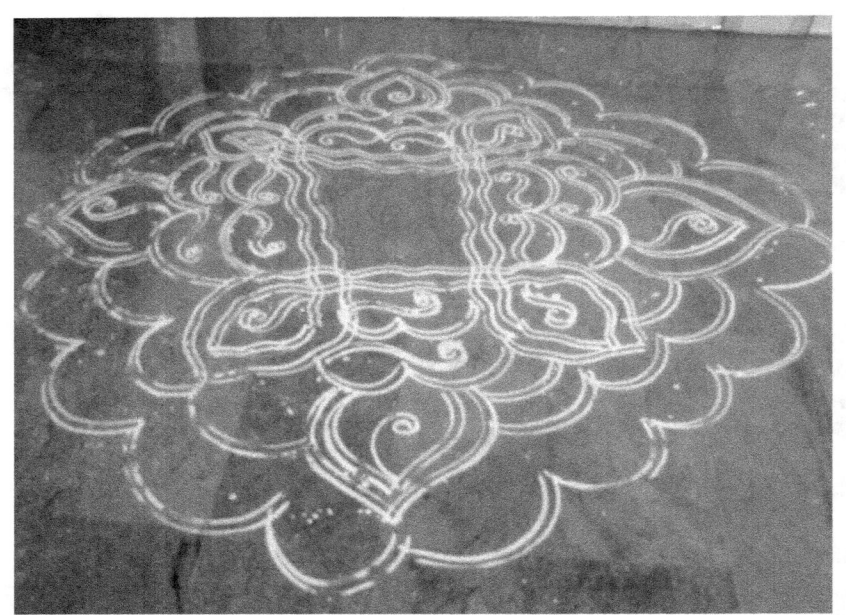

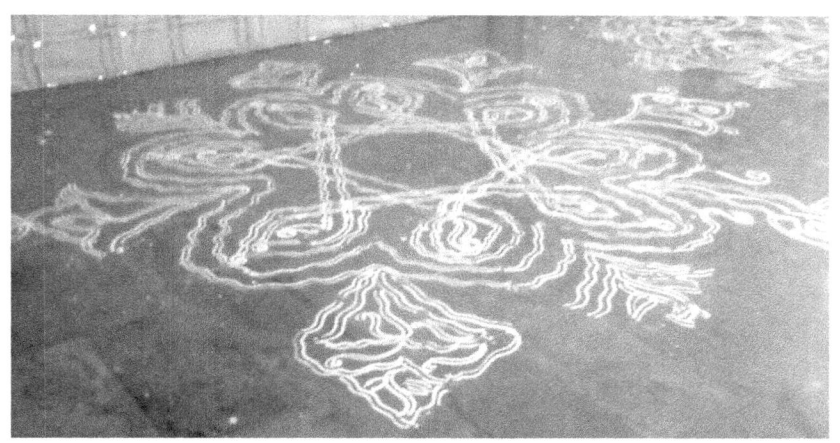

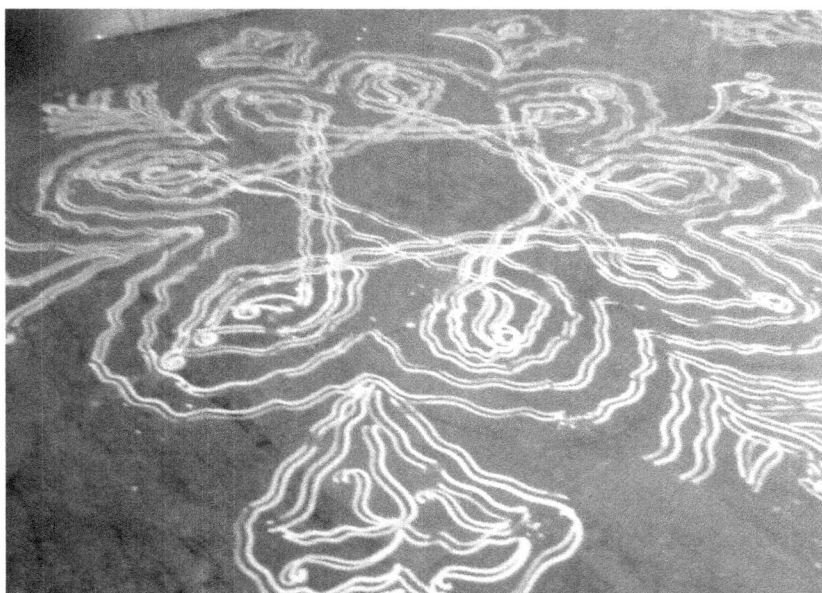

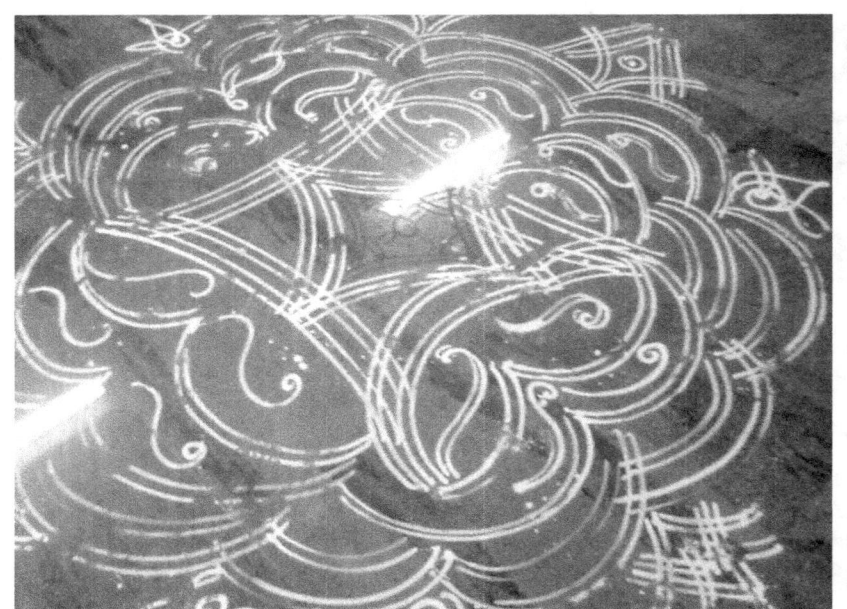

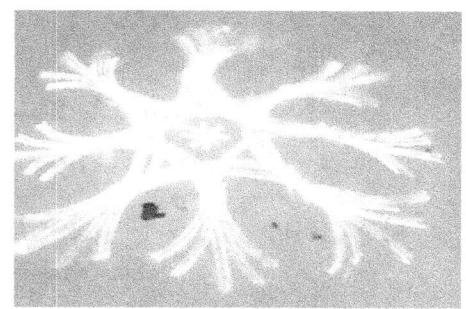

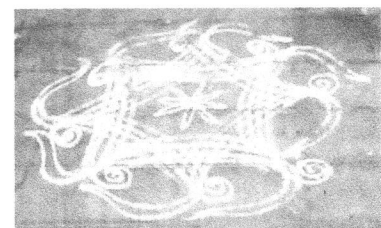

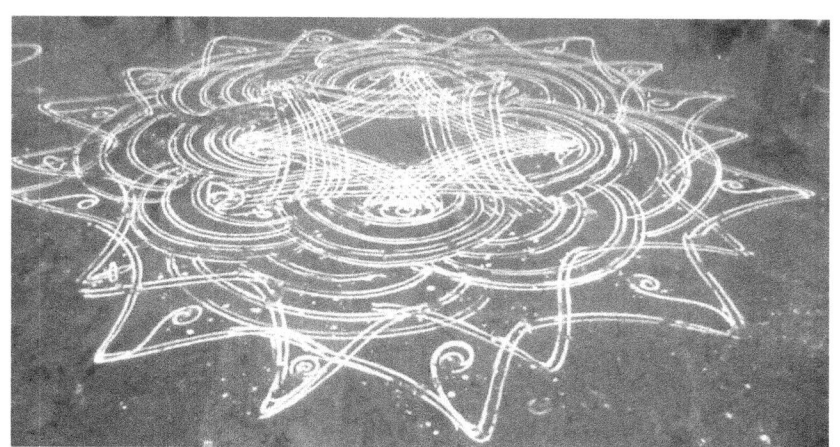

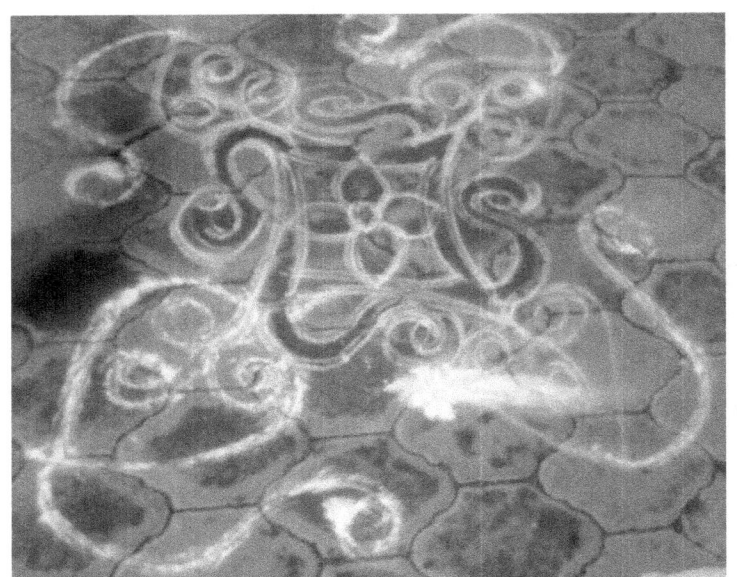

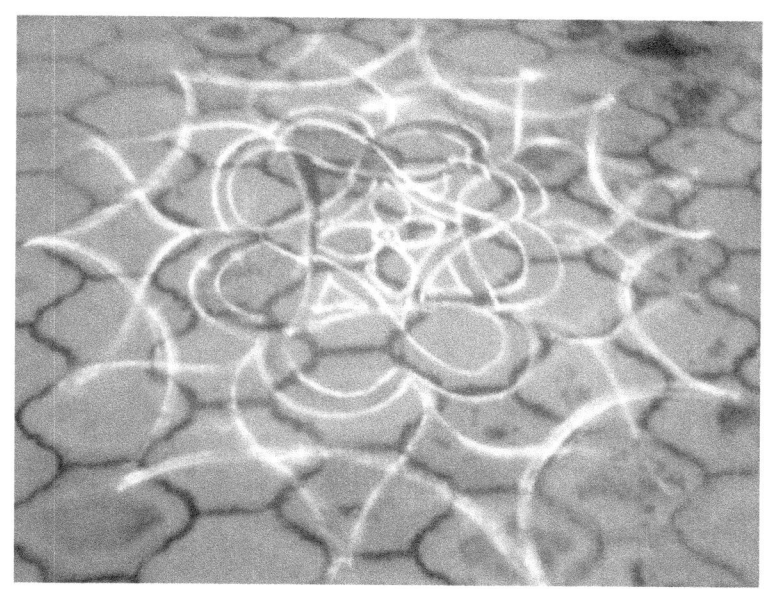

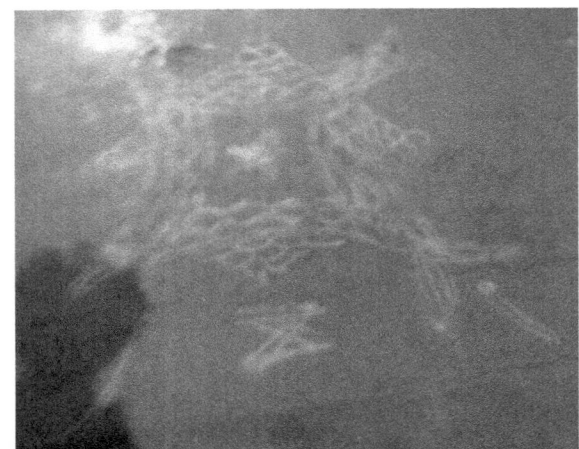

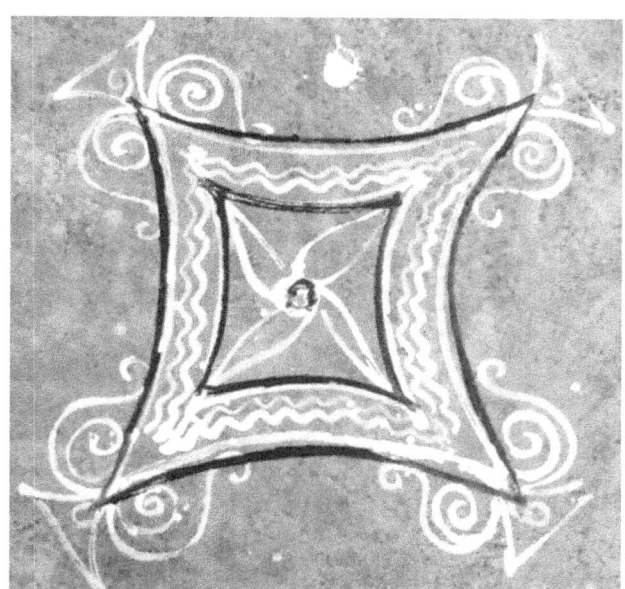

Kolams from unknown artists

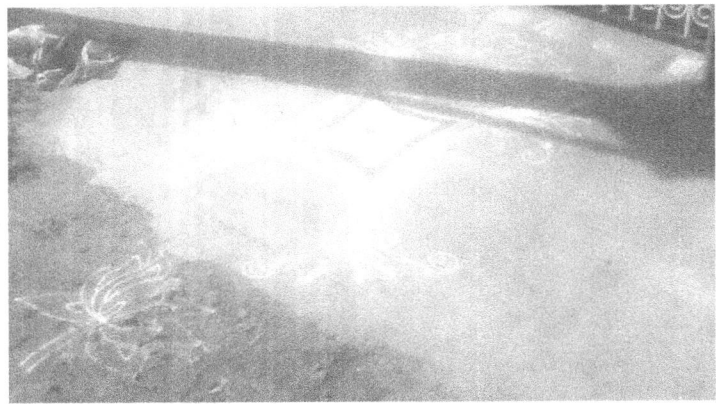

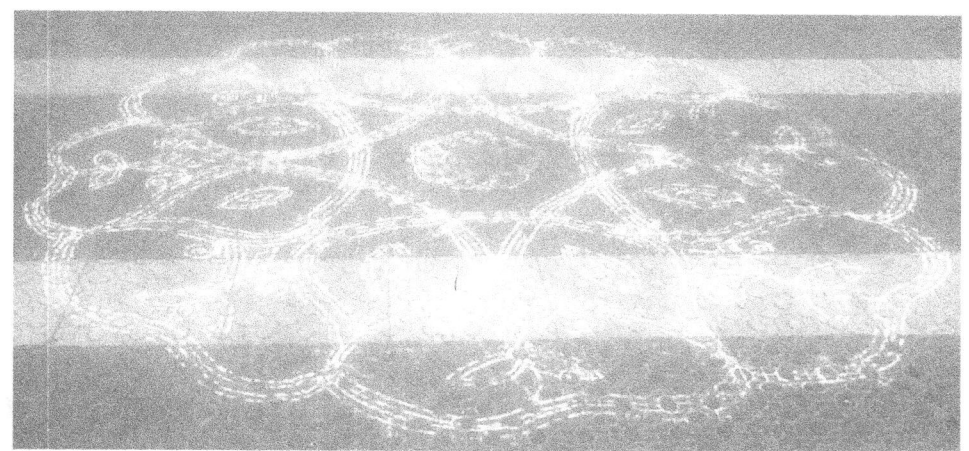

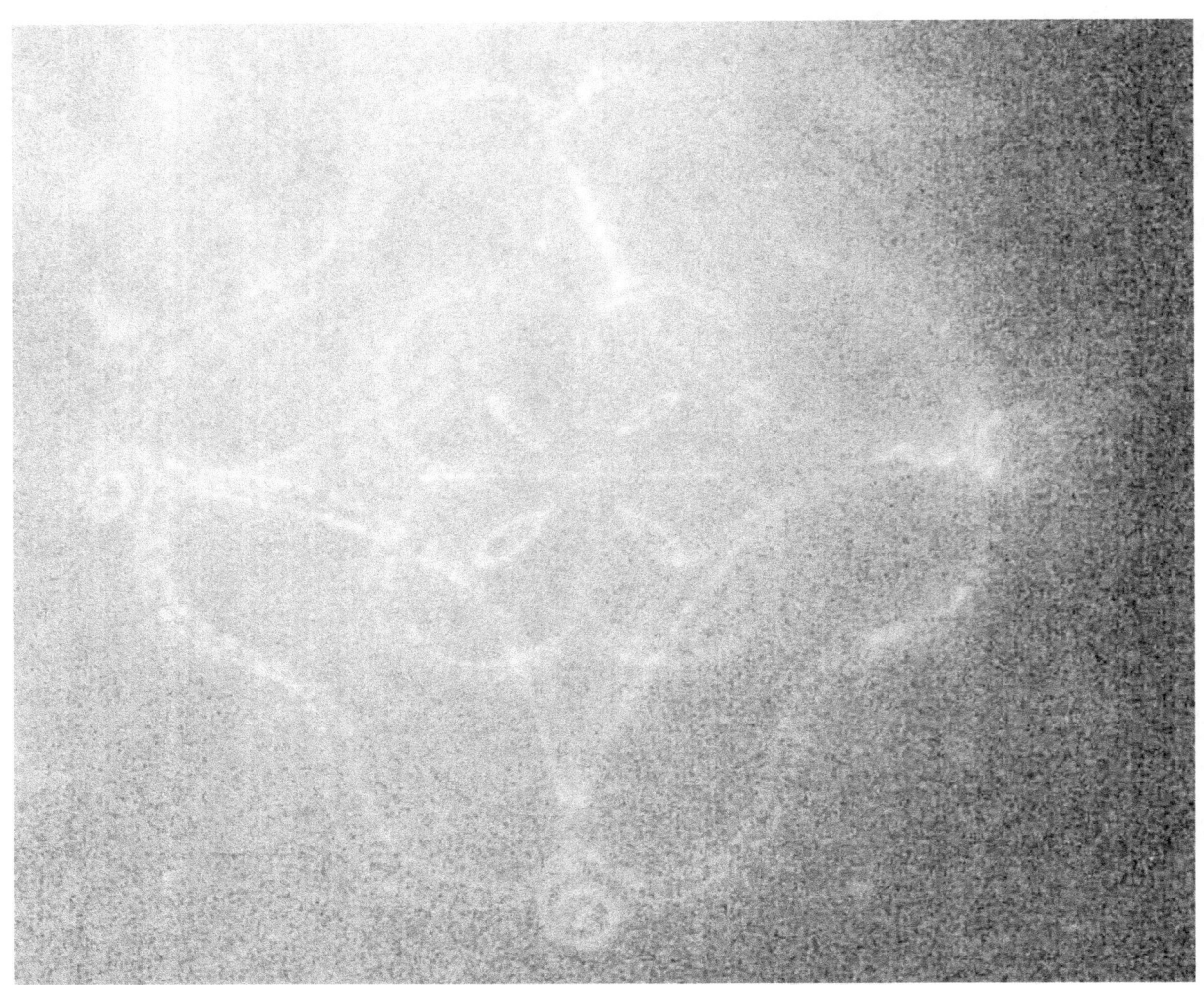

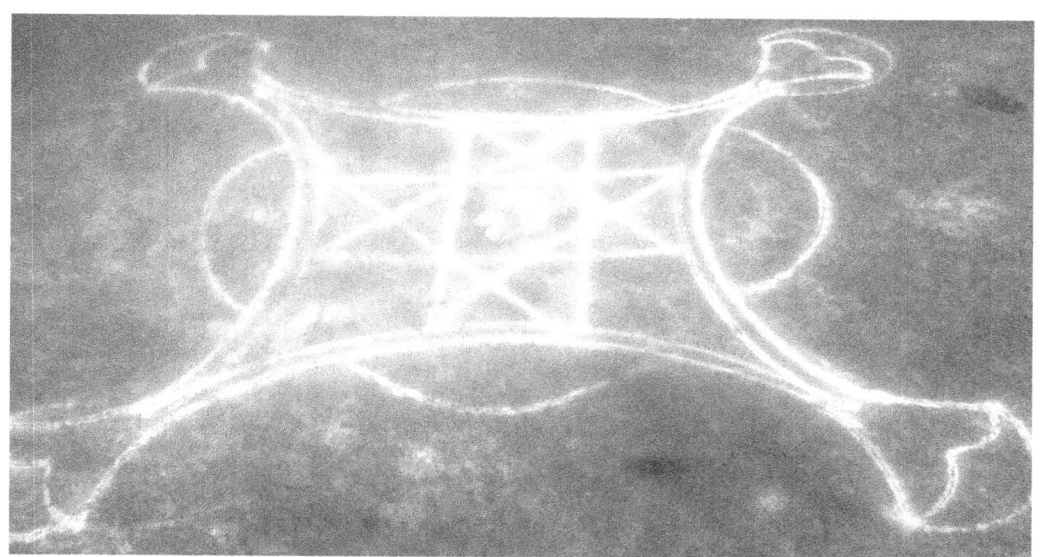

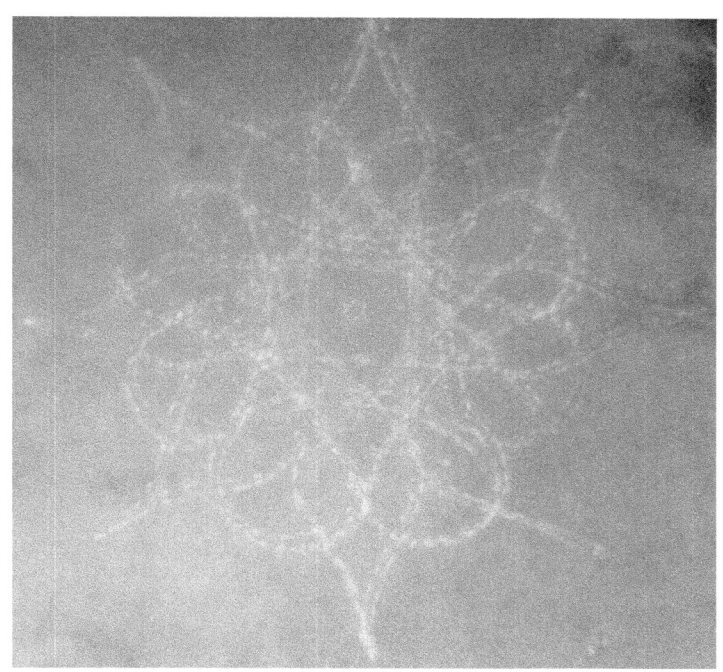

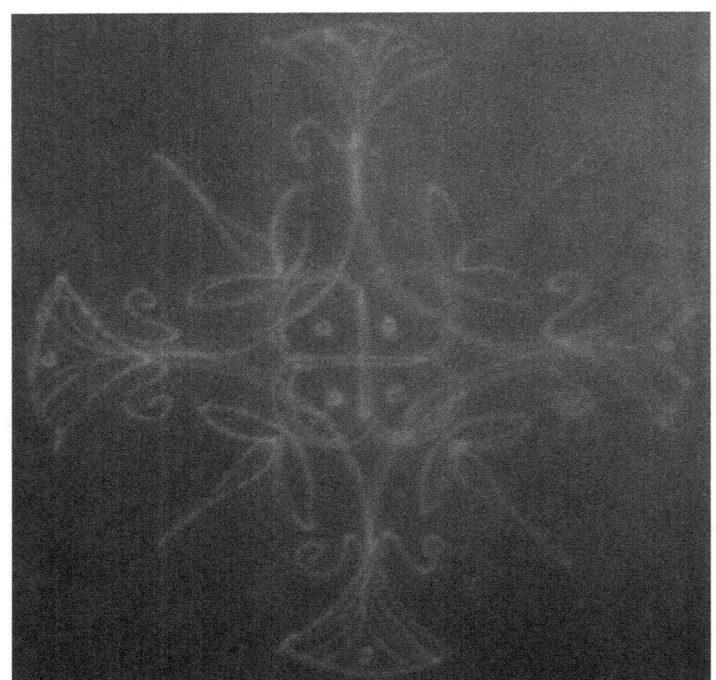

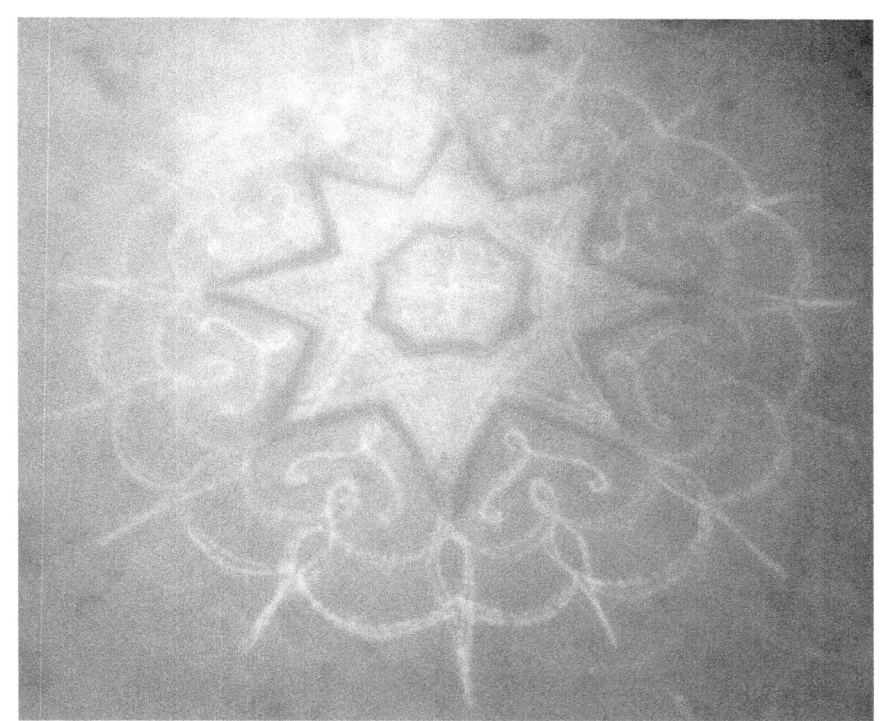

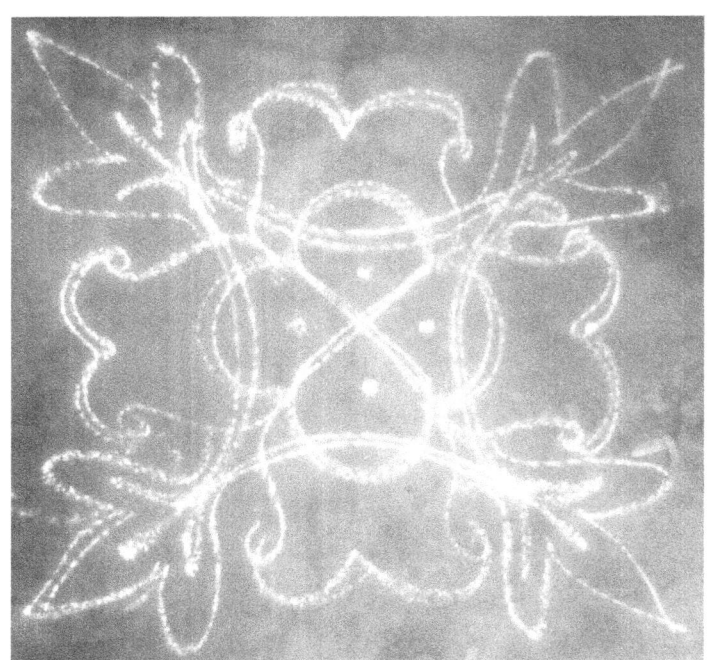

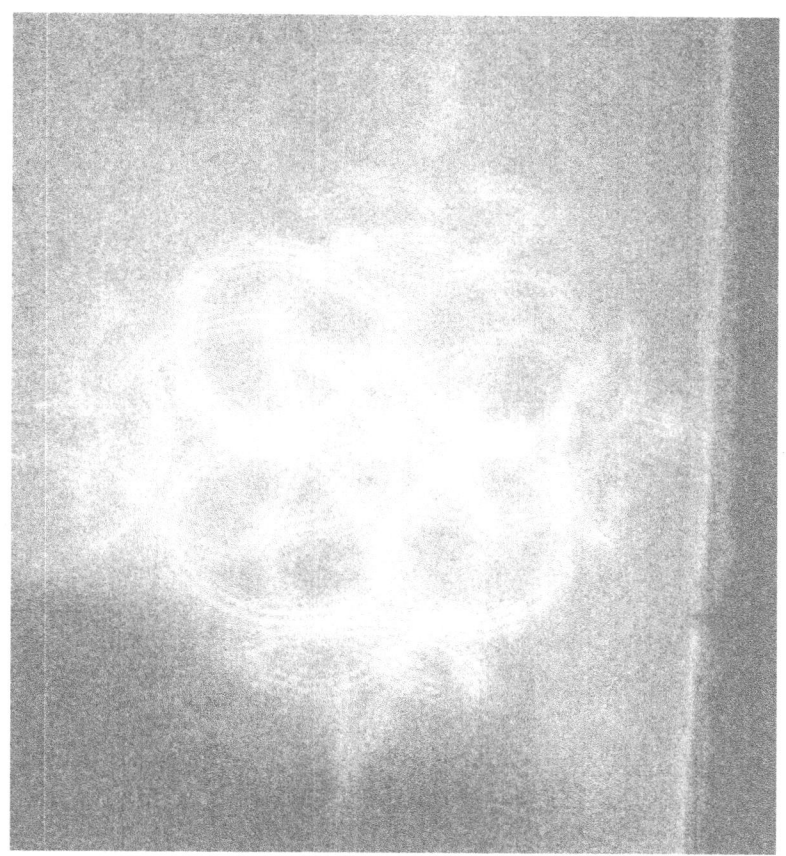

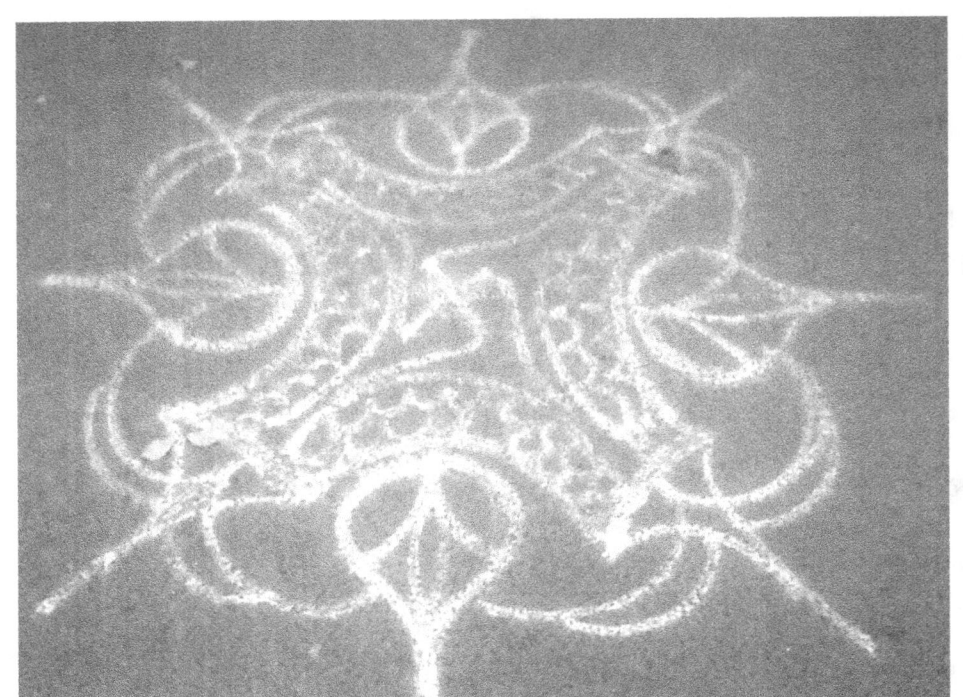

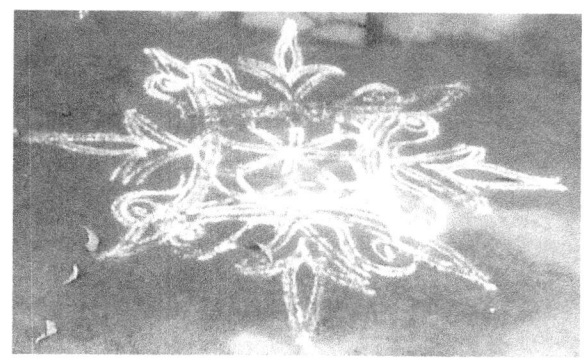

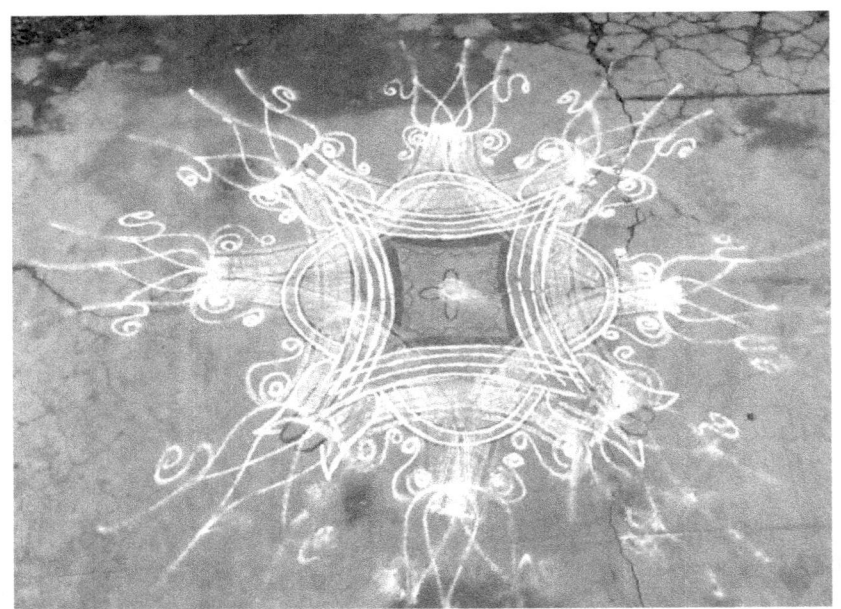

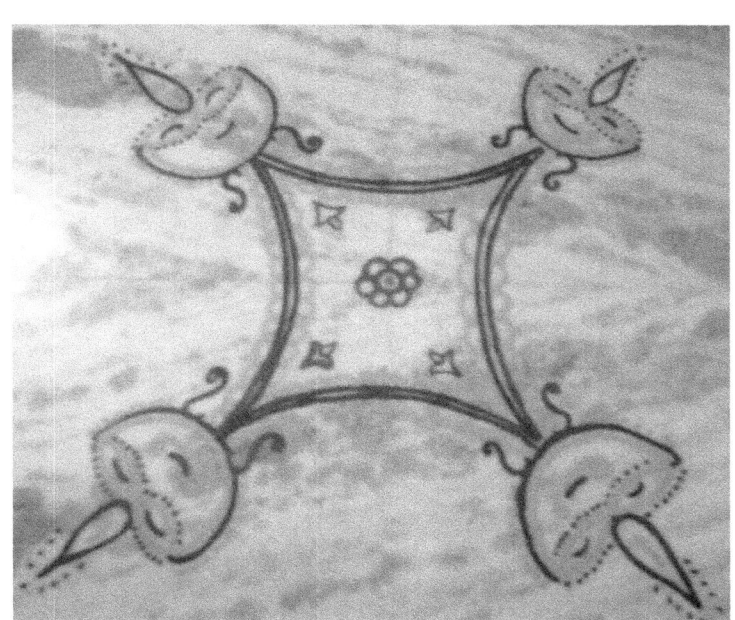

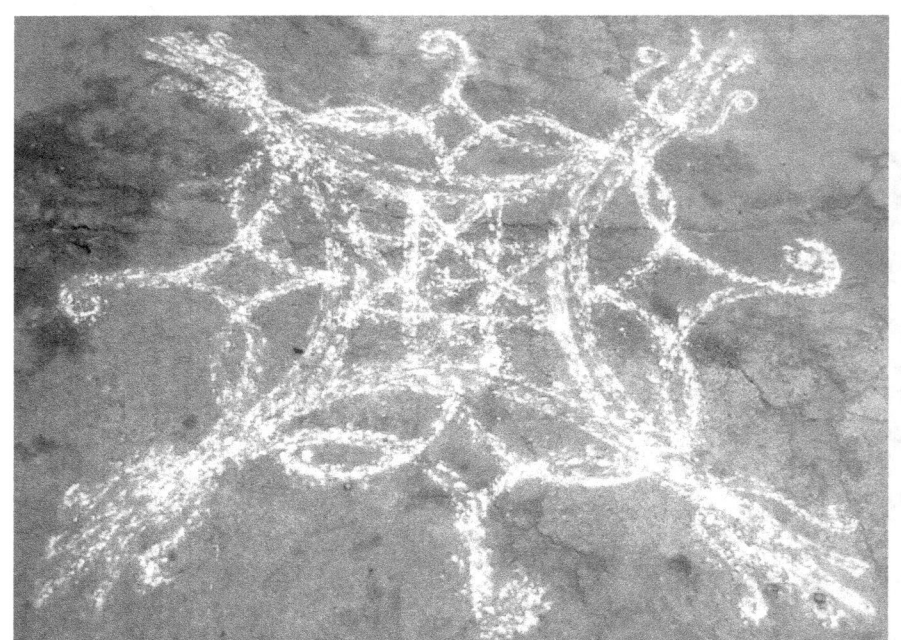

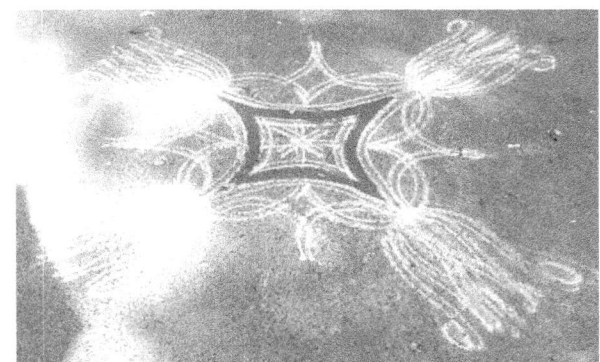

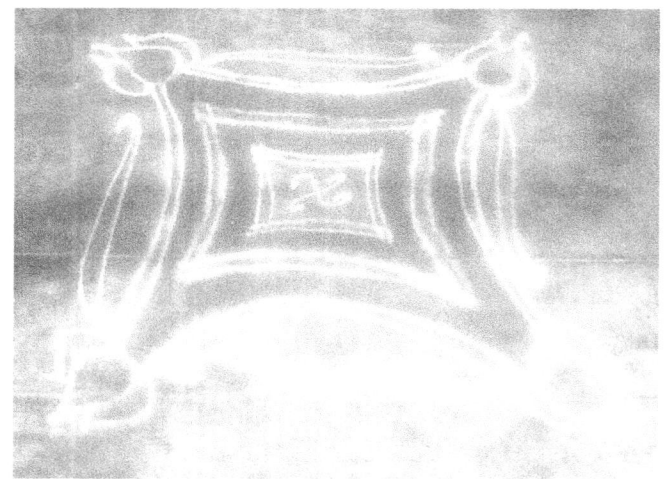

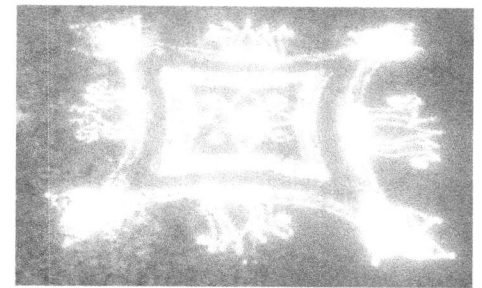

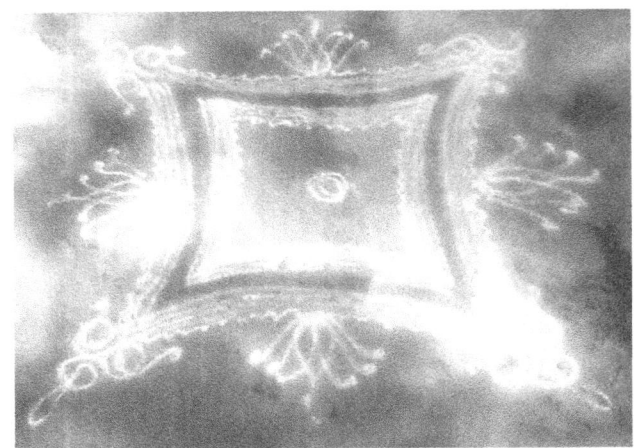

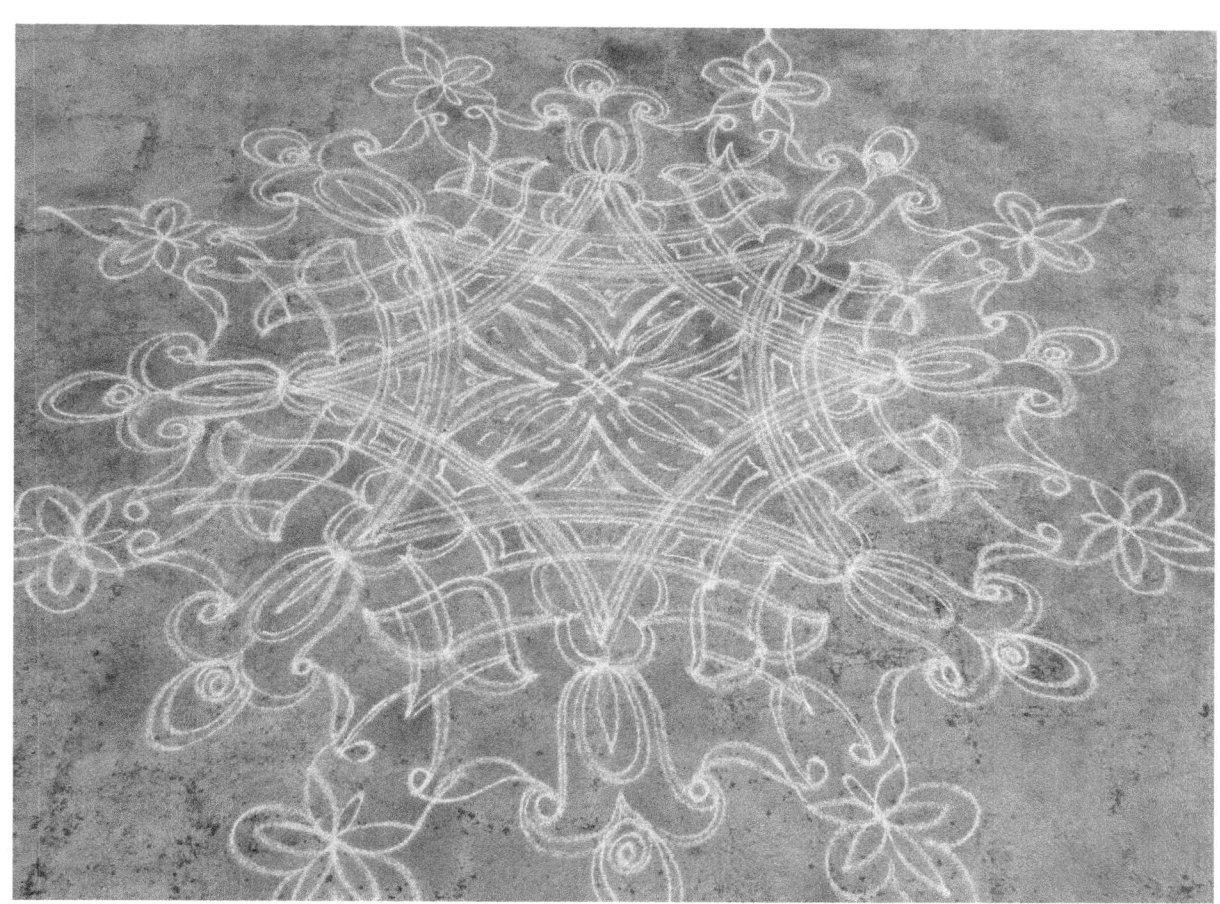

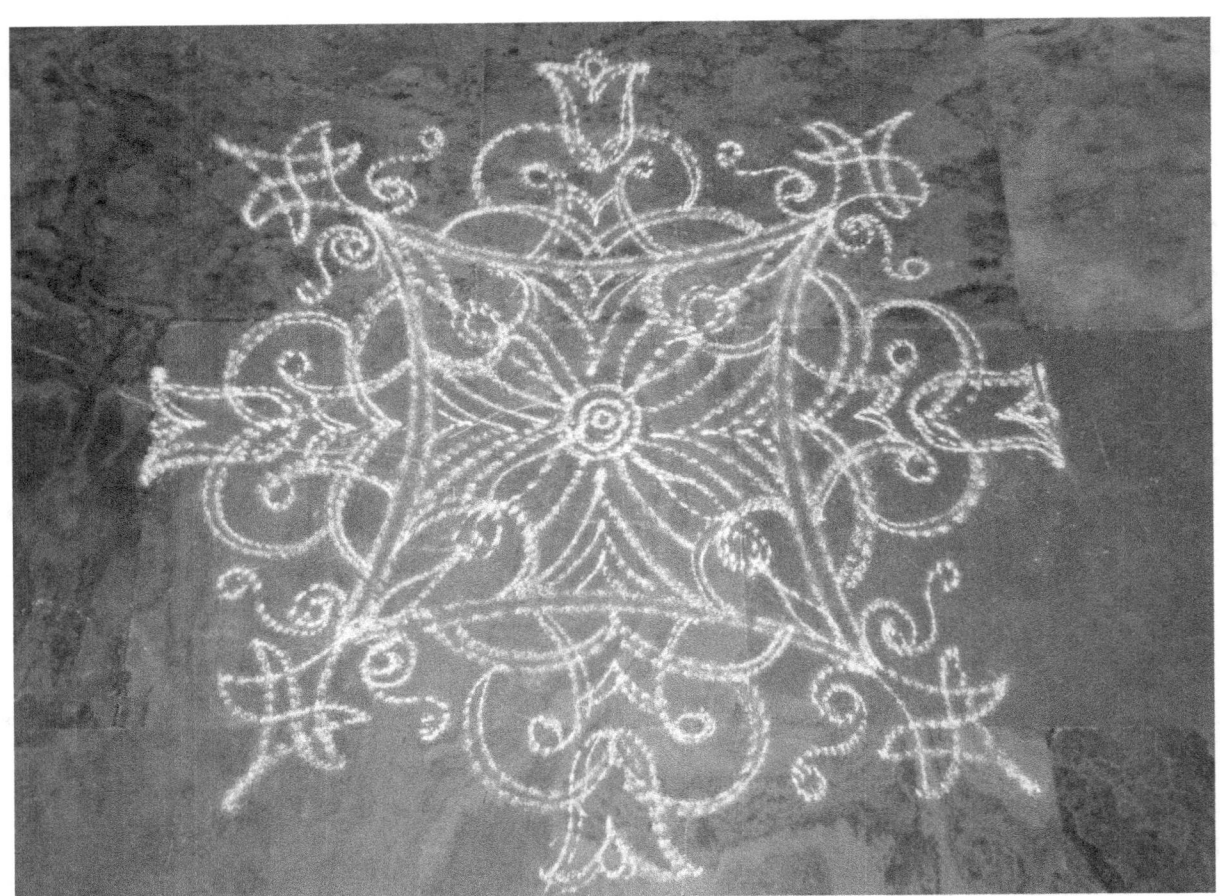

Kolams from unknown artists (Iyer variant of Padi Kolams)

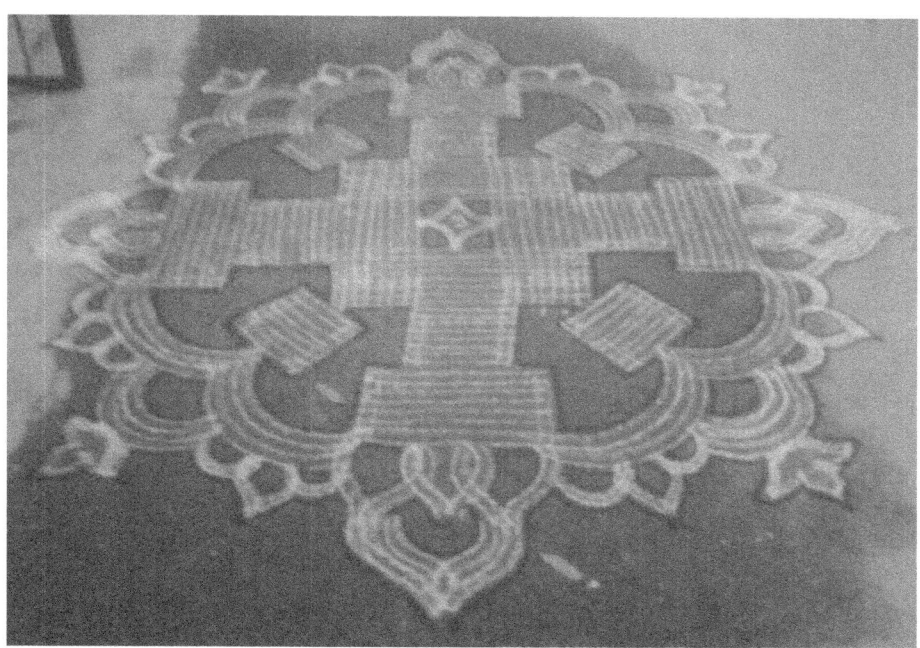

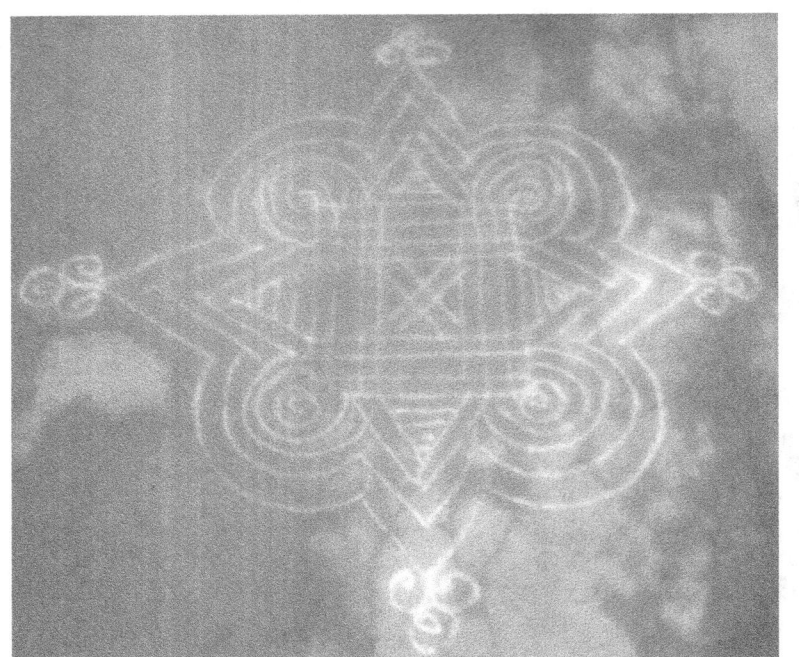

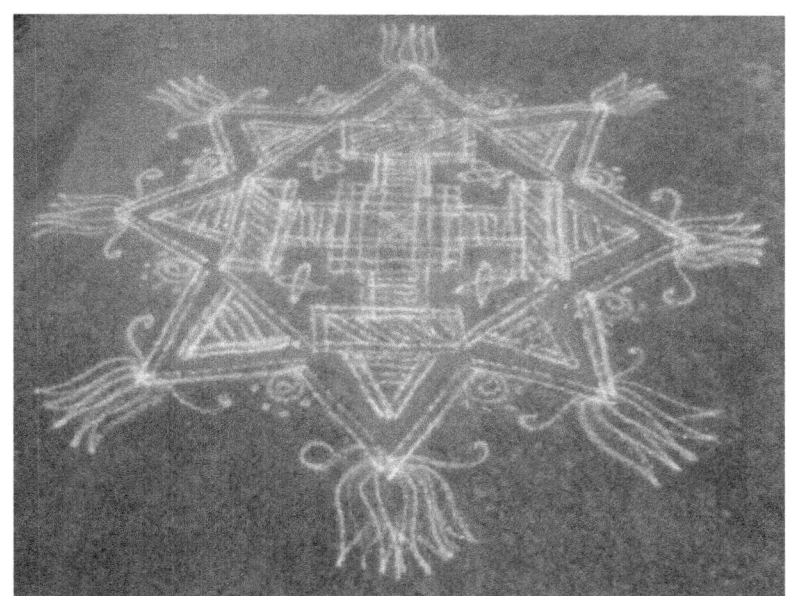

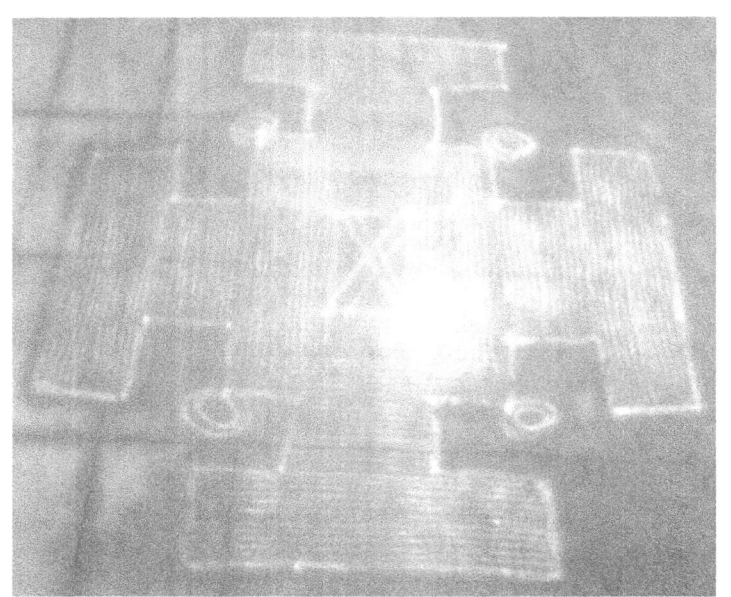

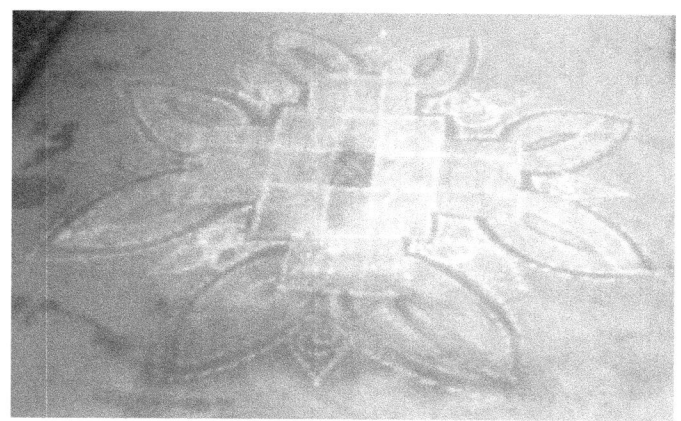

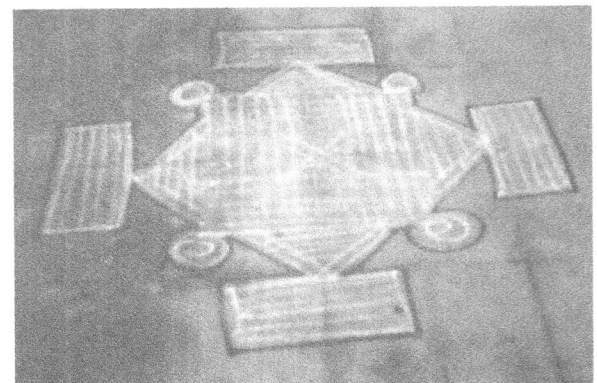

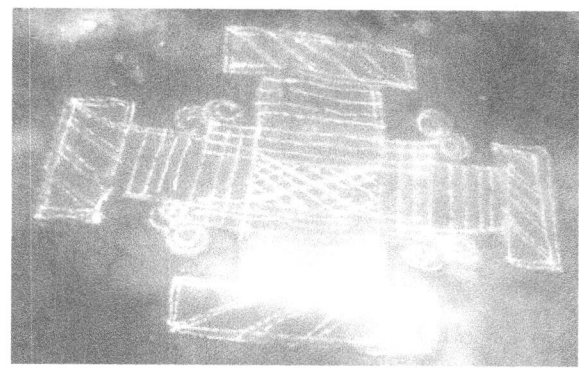

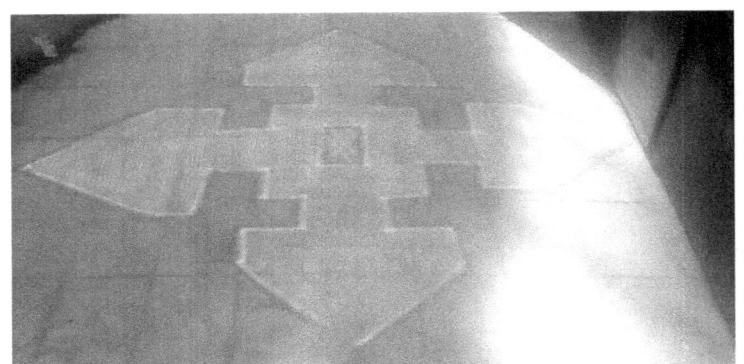

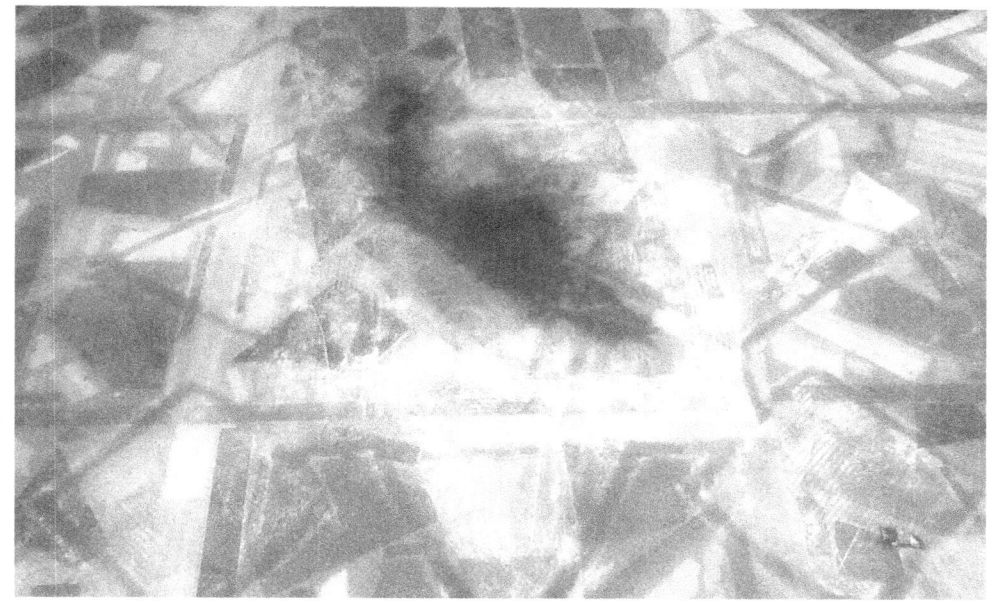

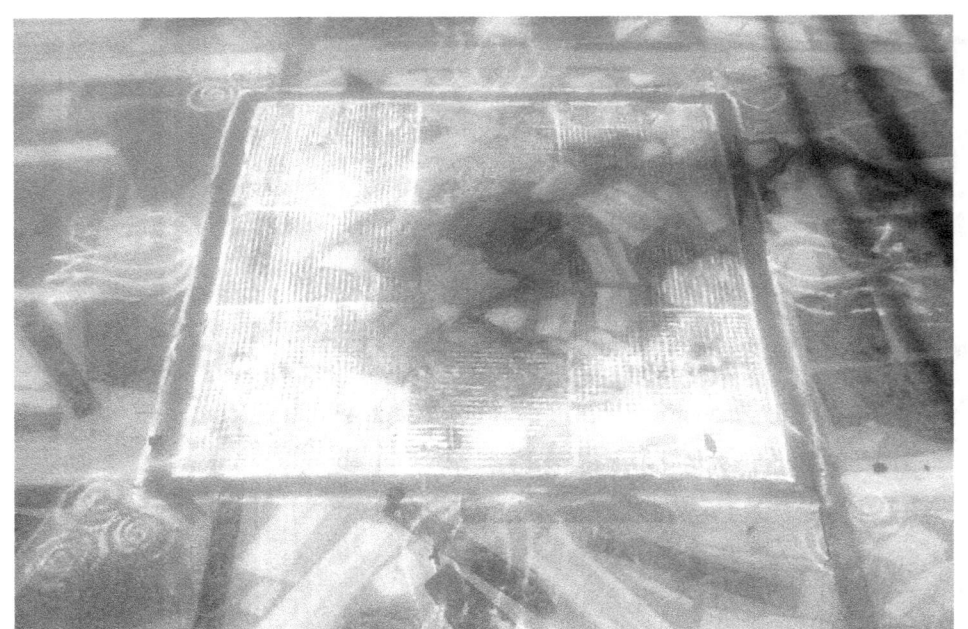

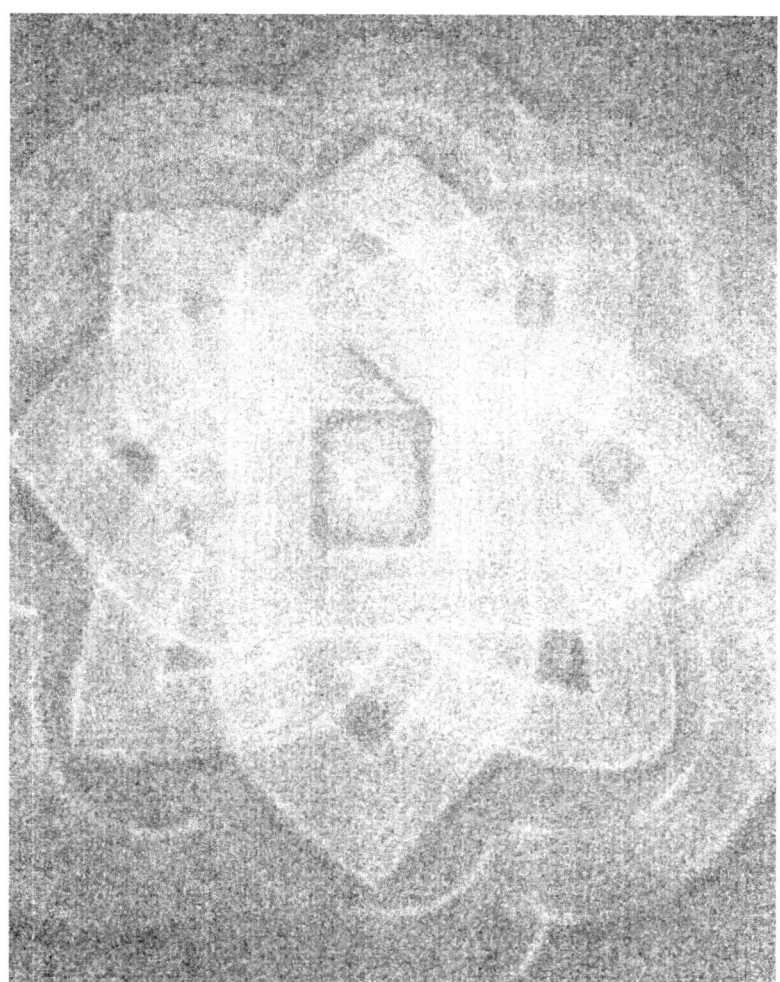

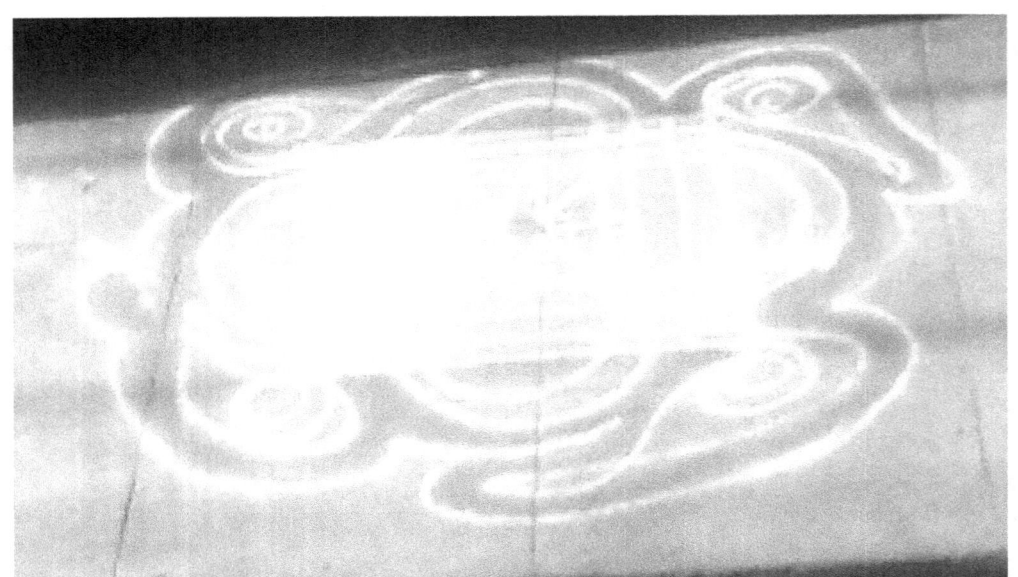

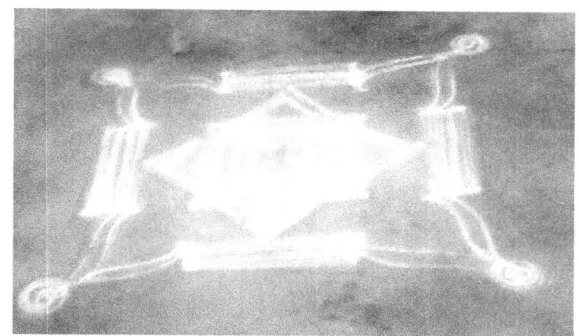

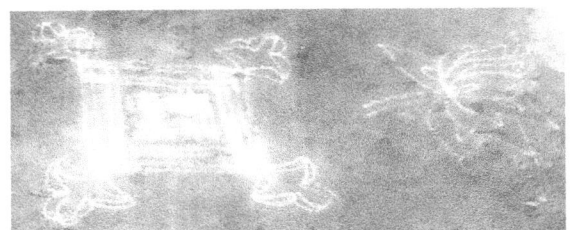

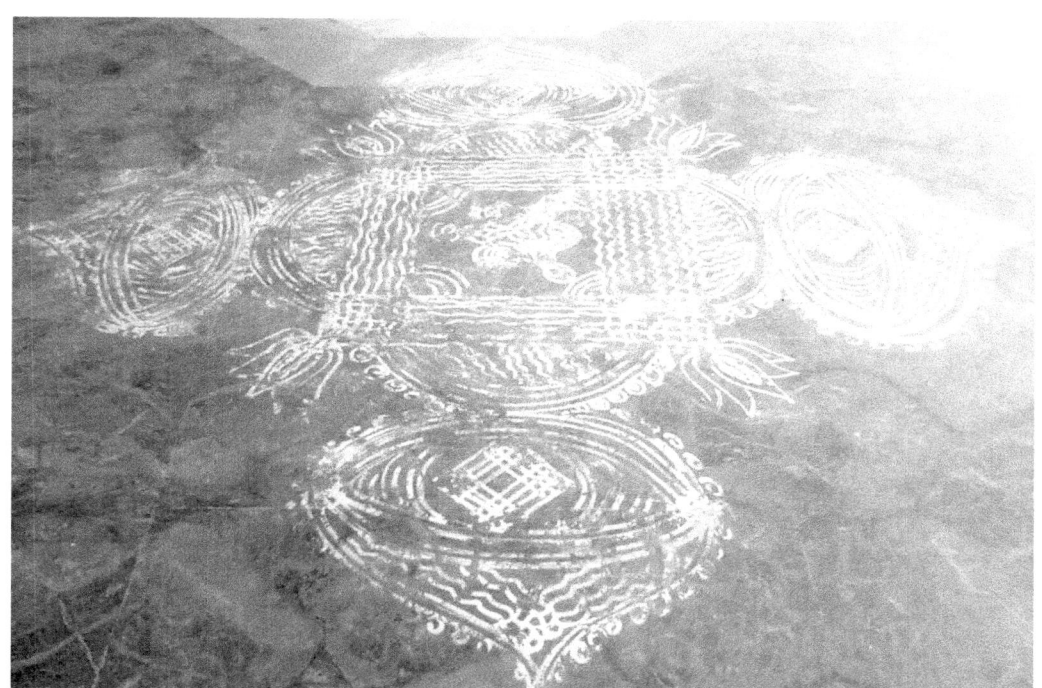

Guess whos this could be ☺ ?

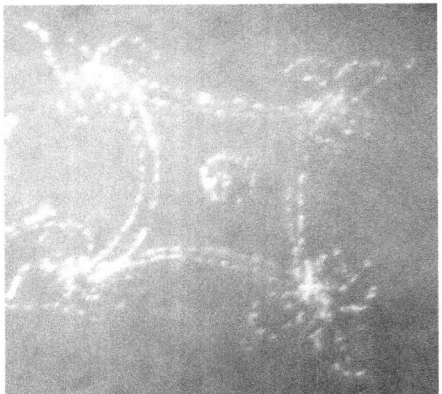

Non Padi Kolams

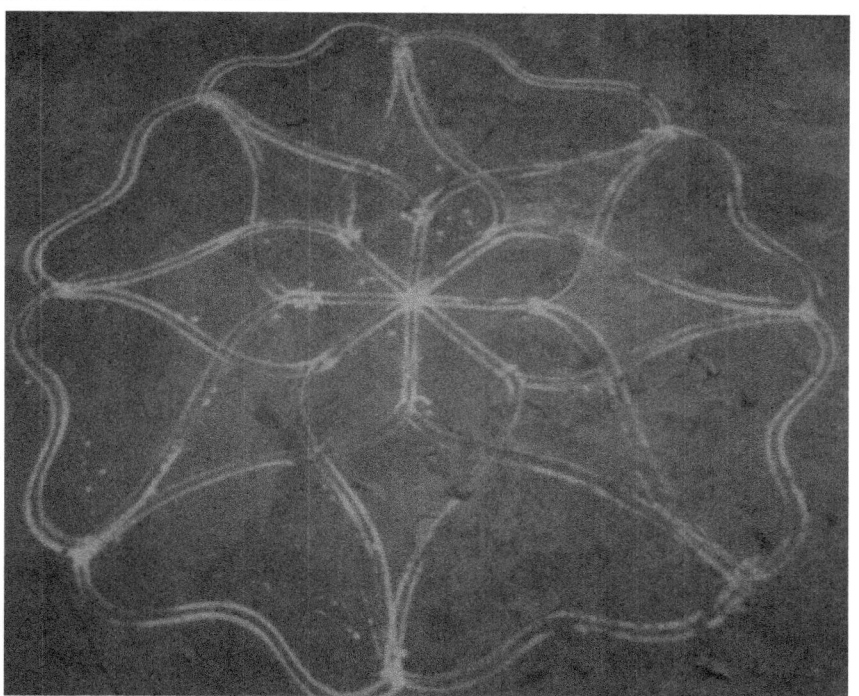

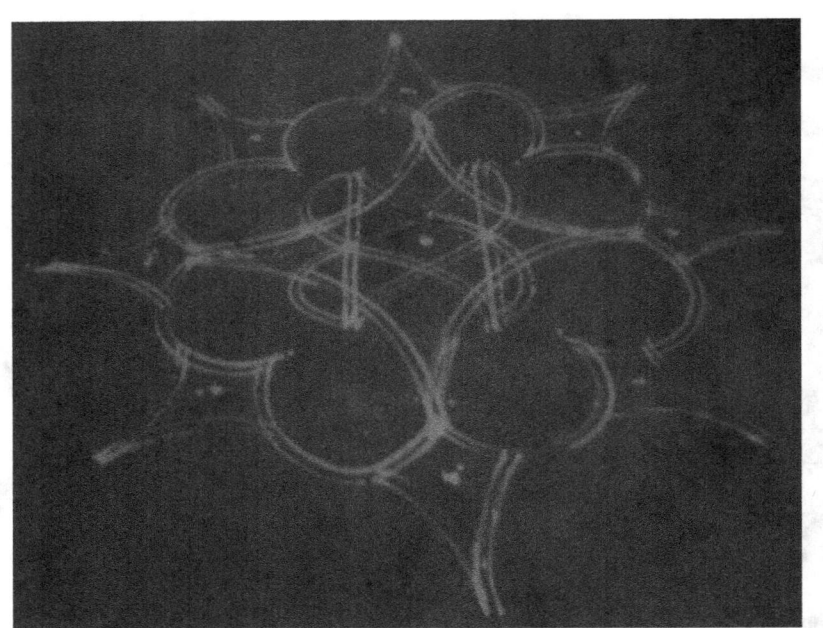

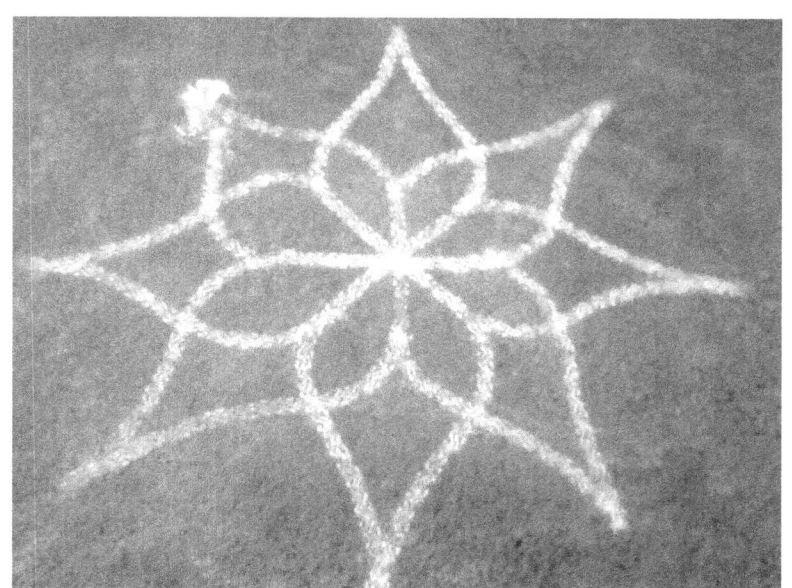

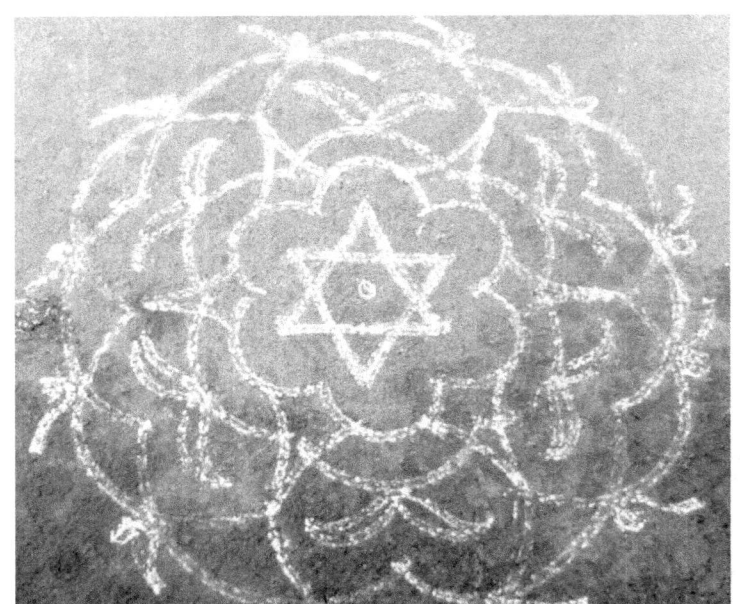

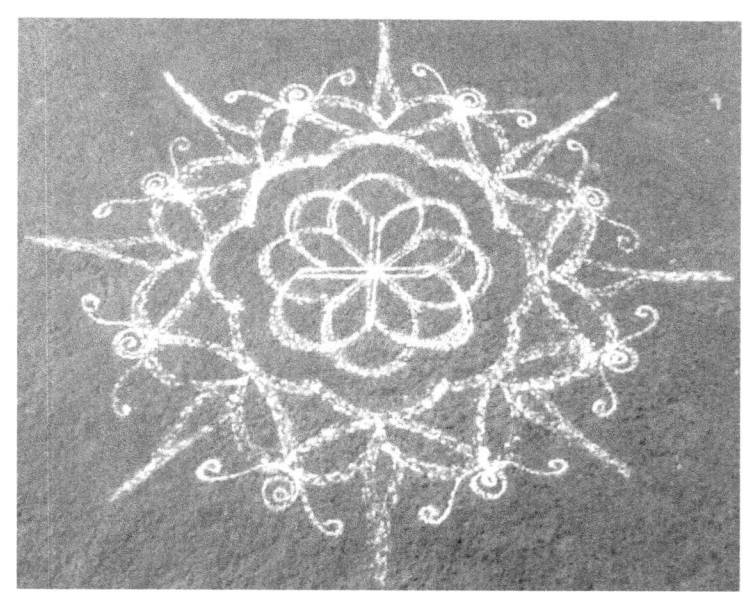

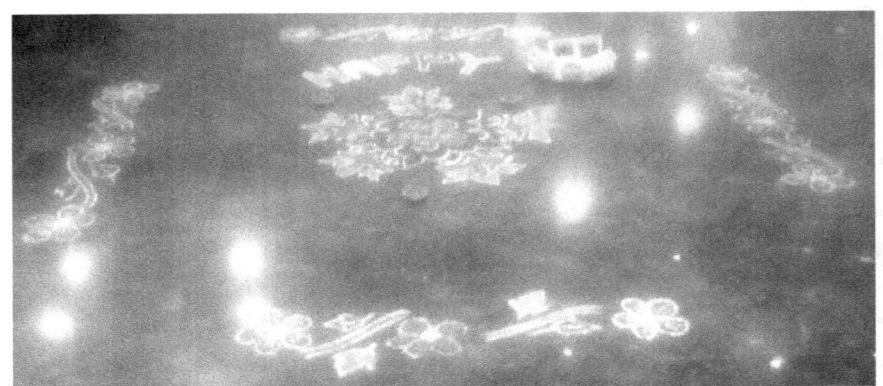

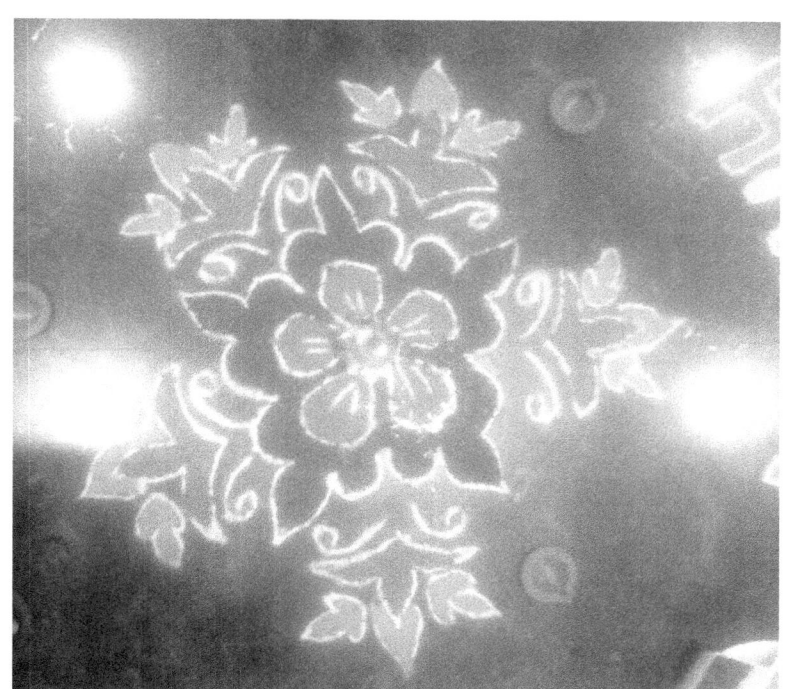

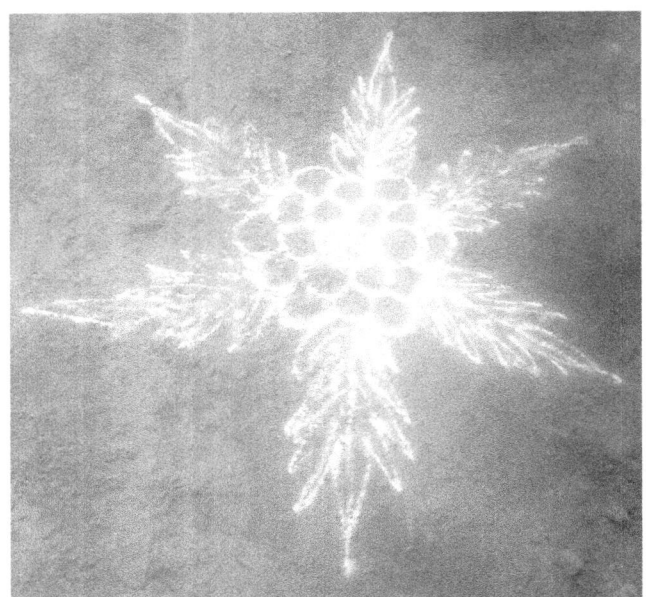

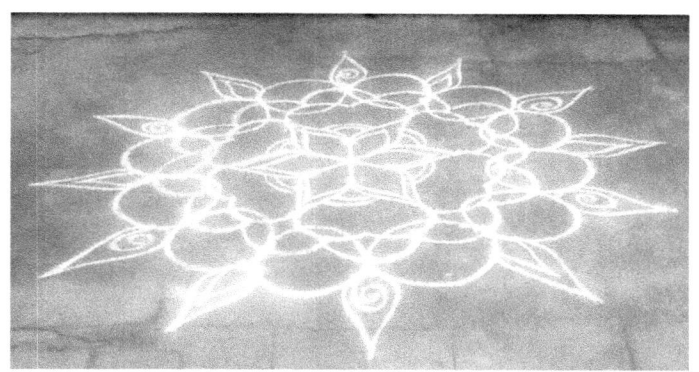

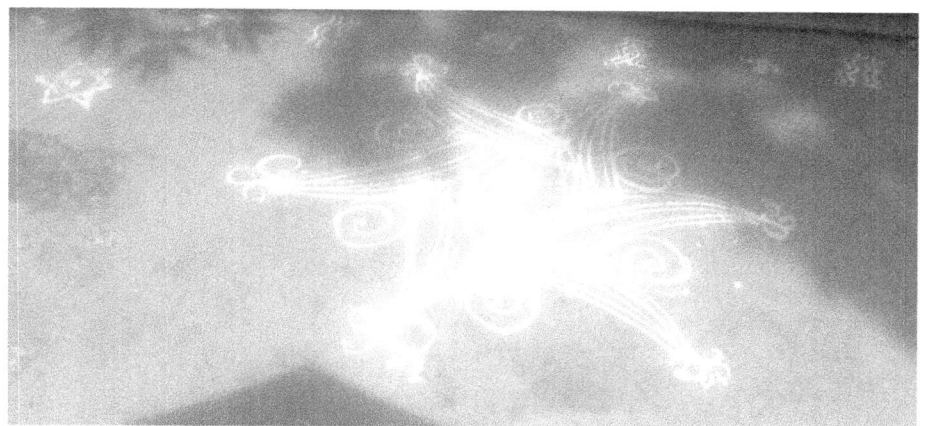

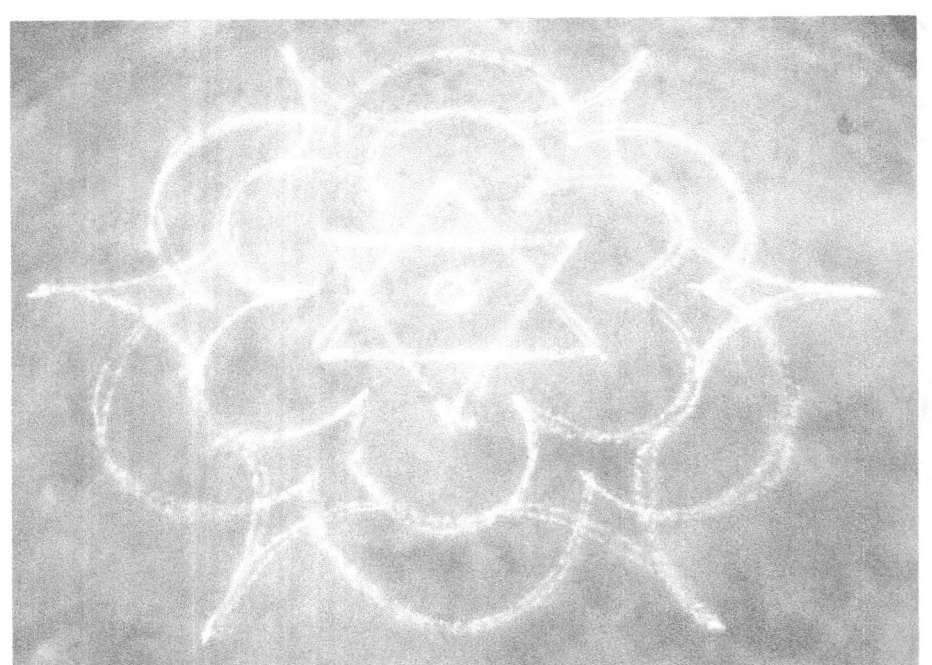

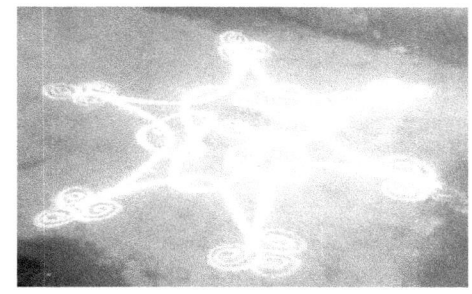

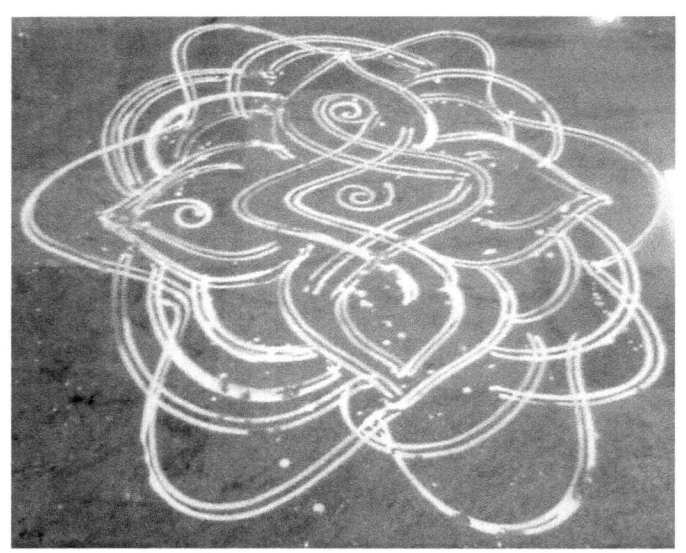

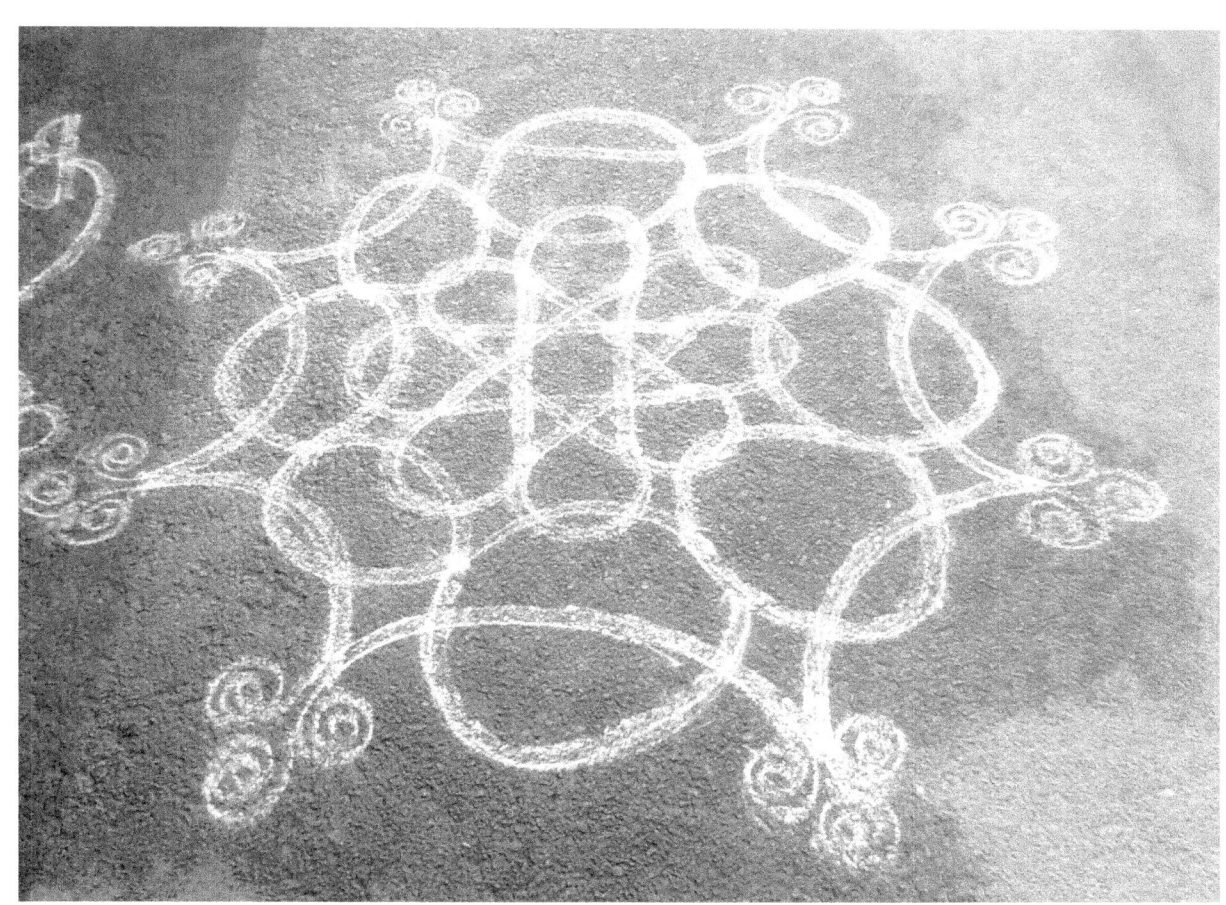

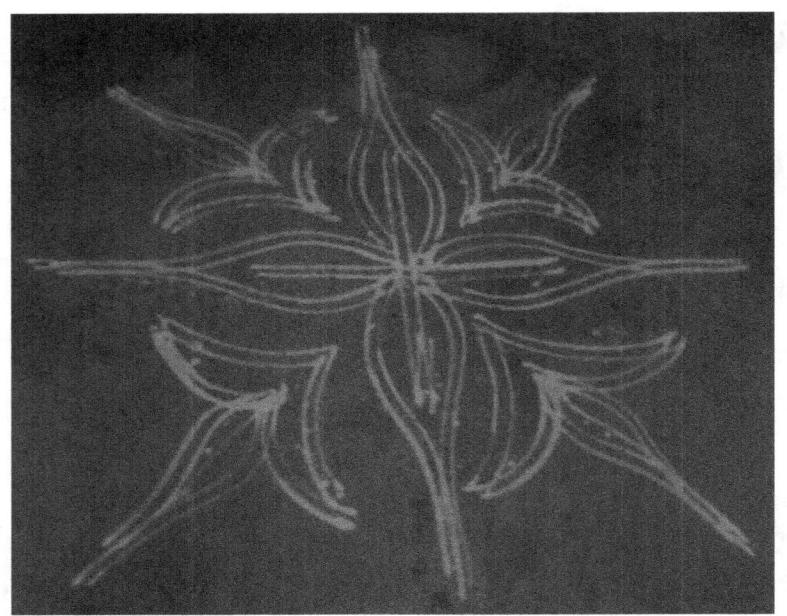

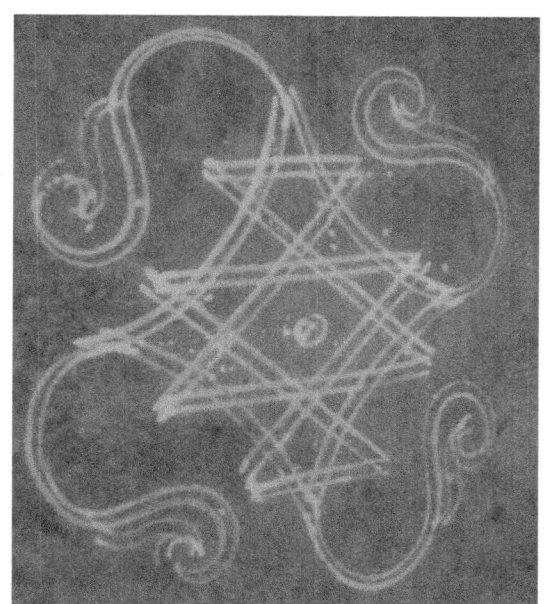

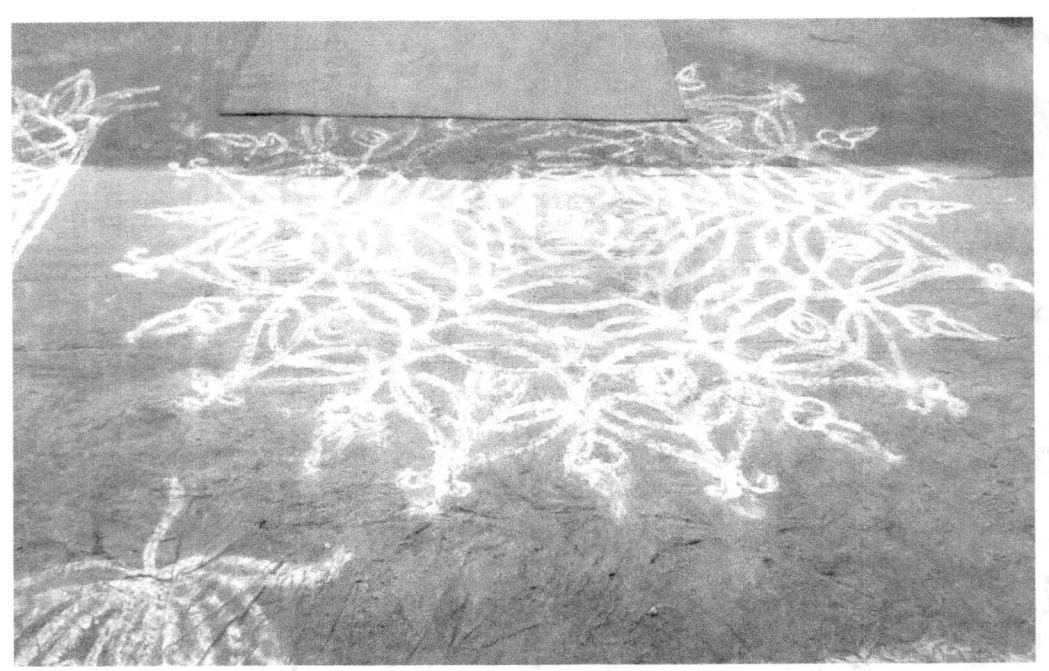

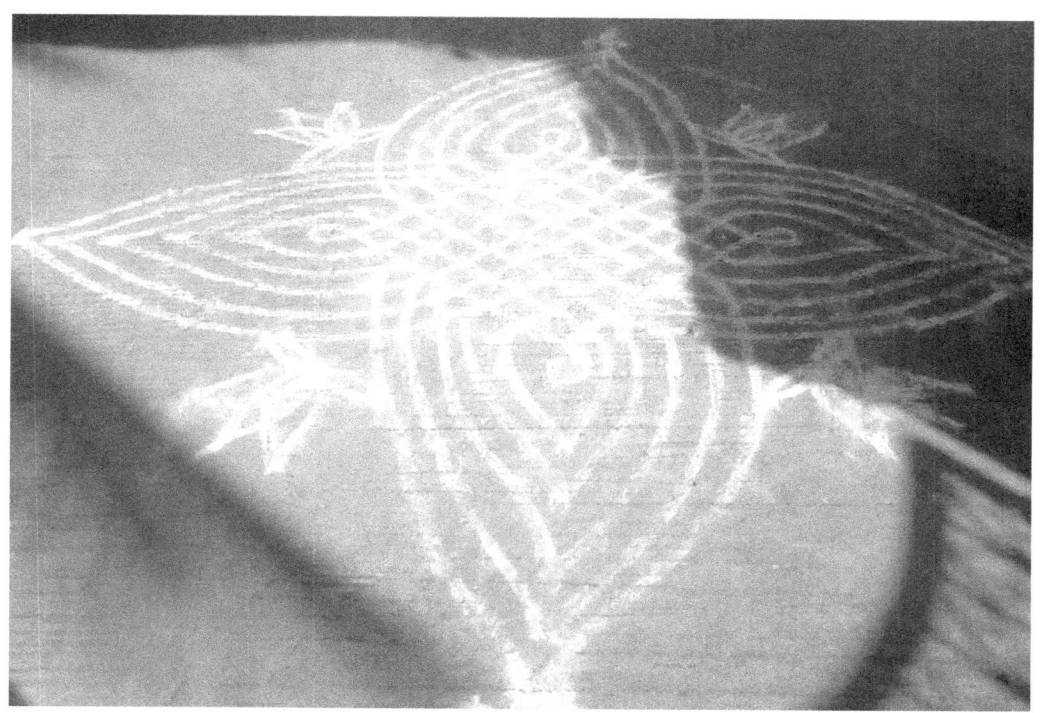

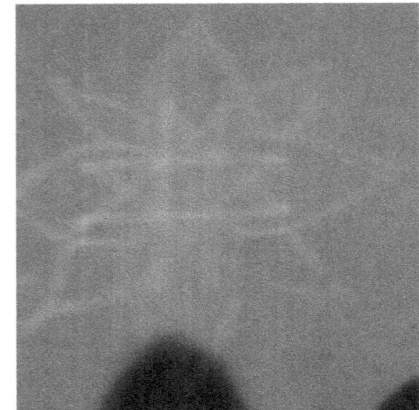

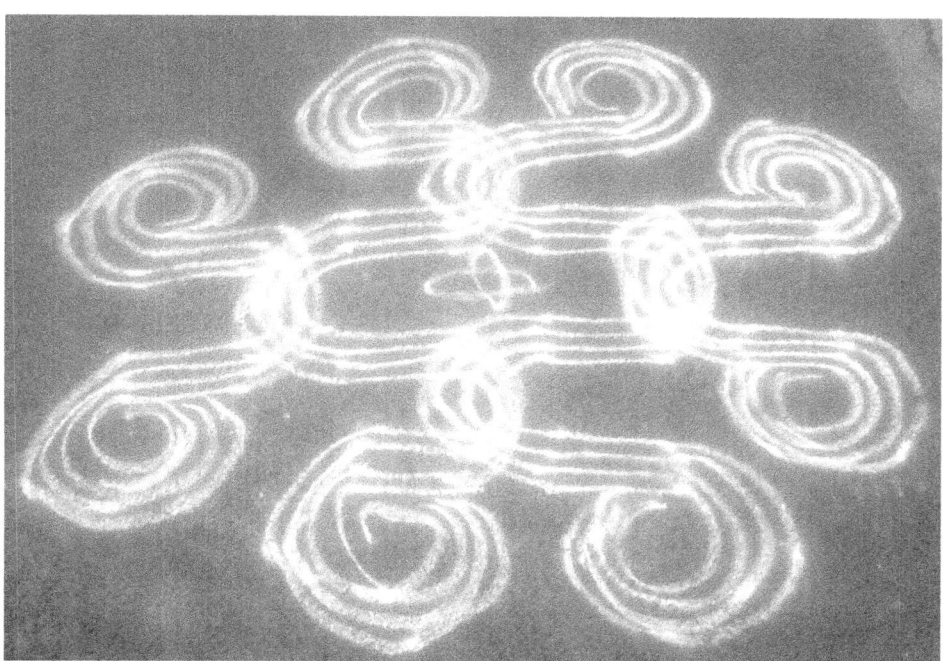

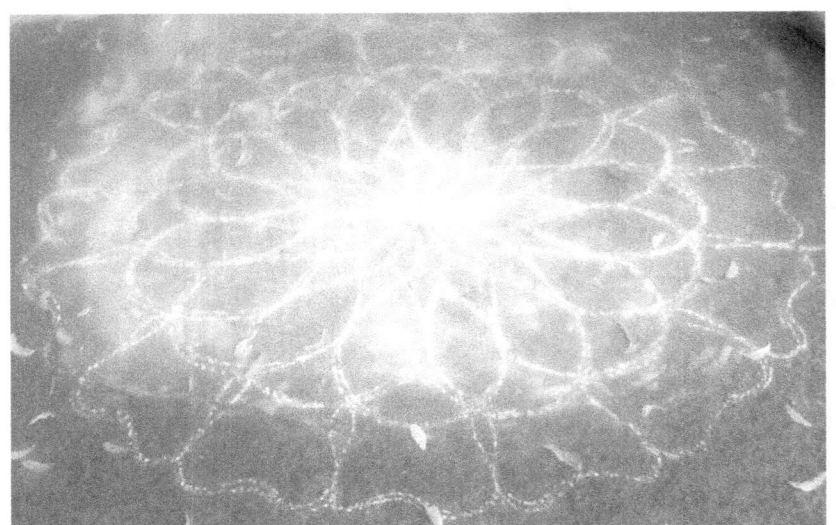

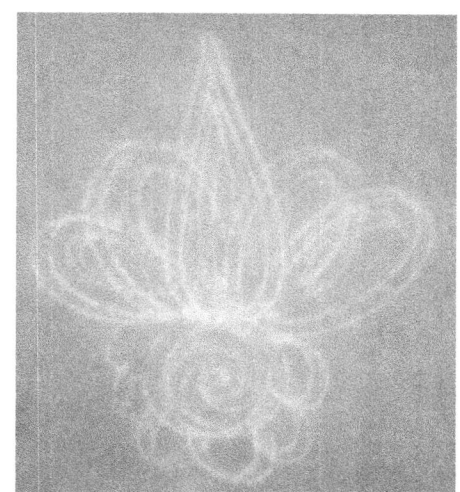

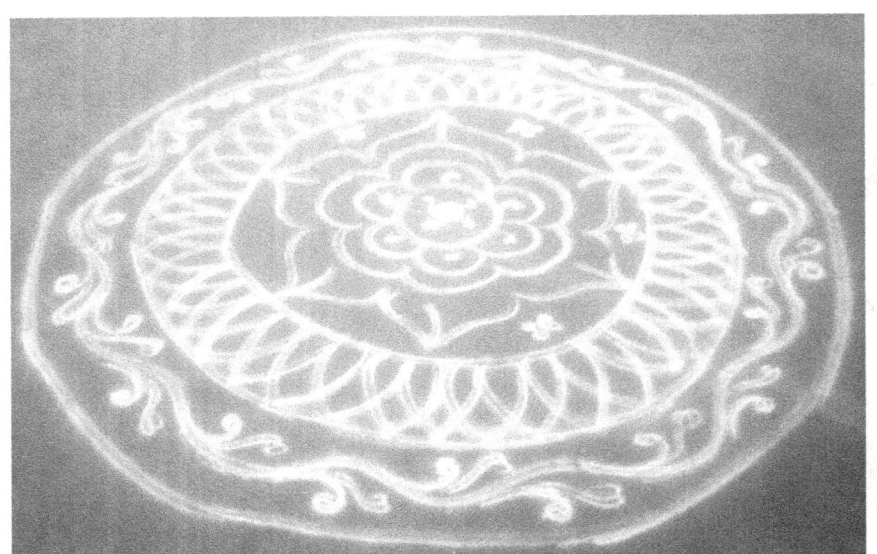

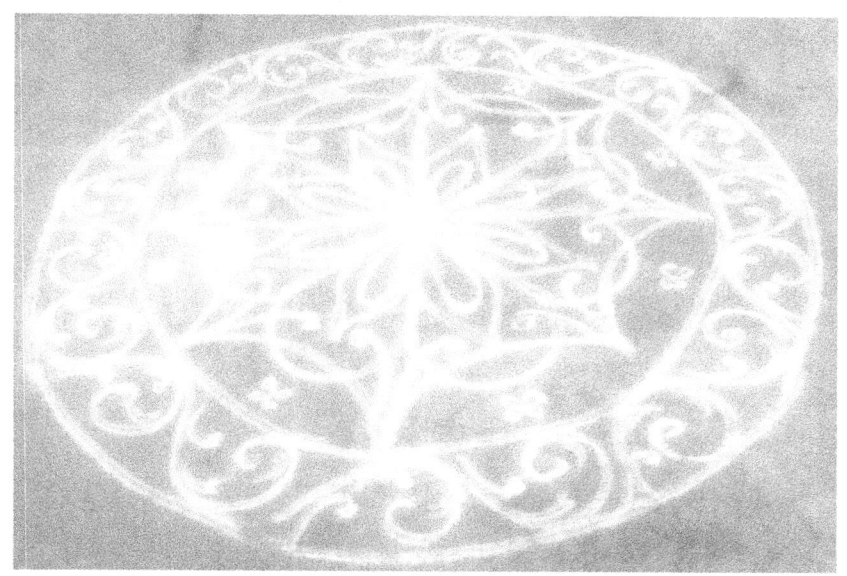

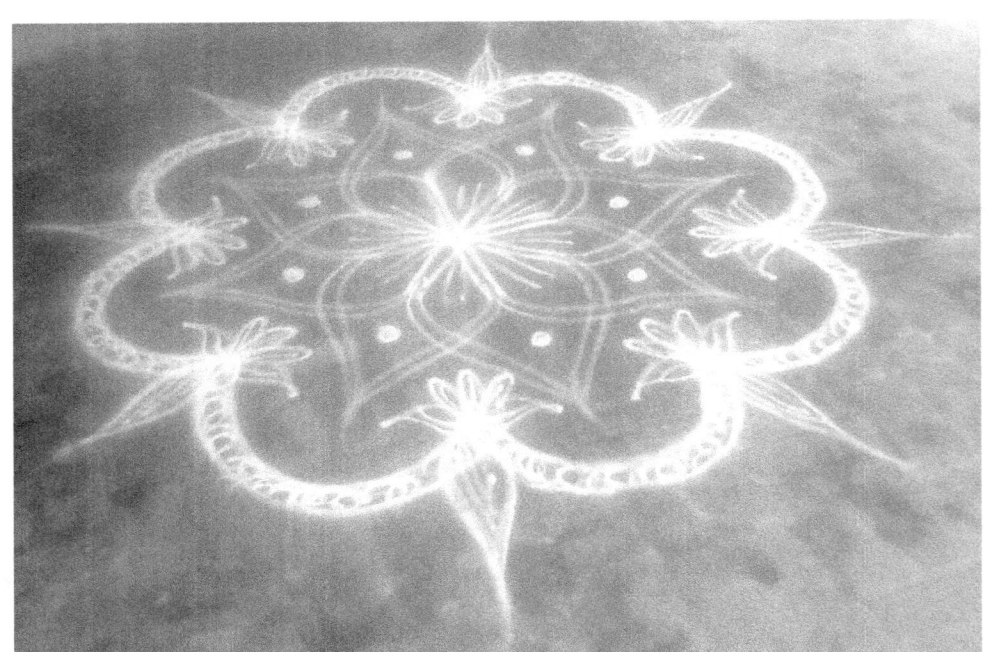

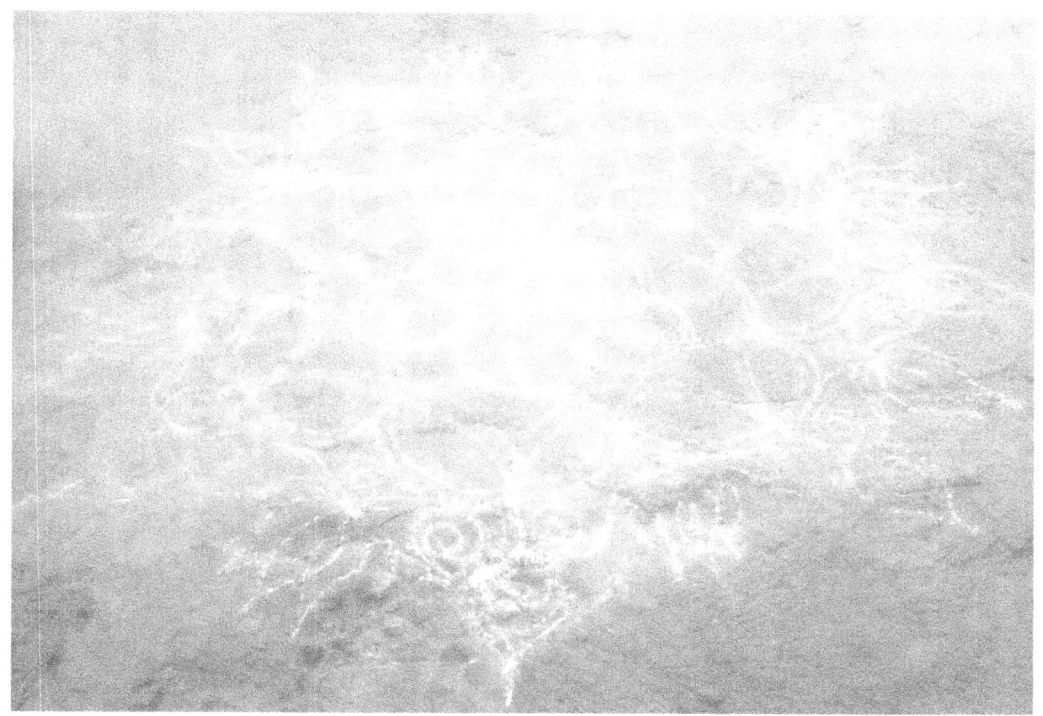

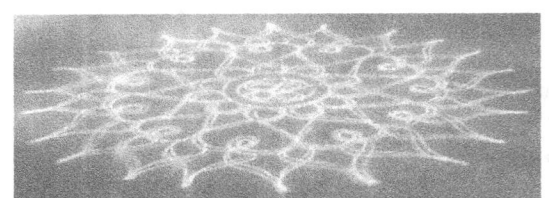

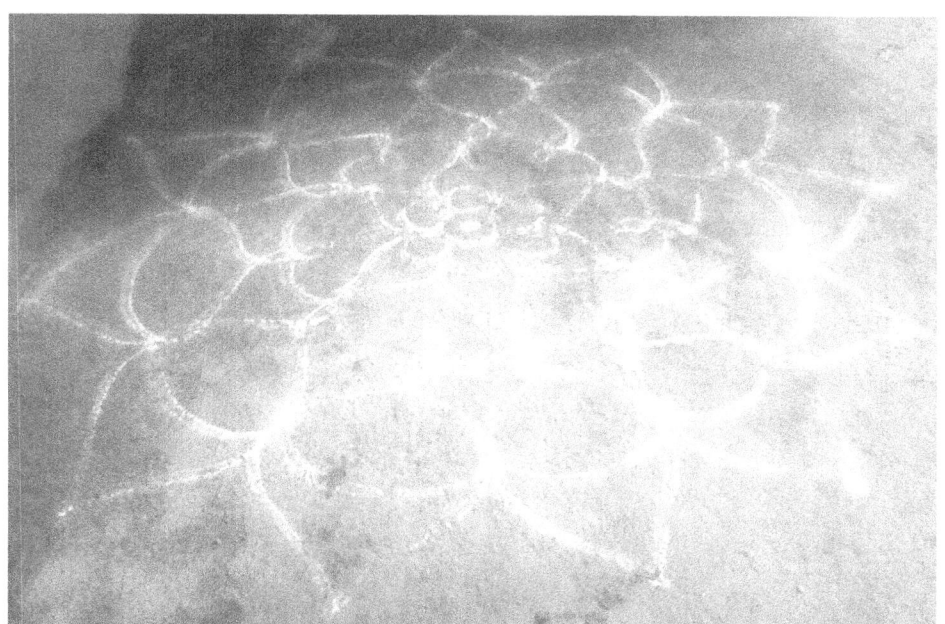

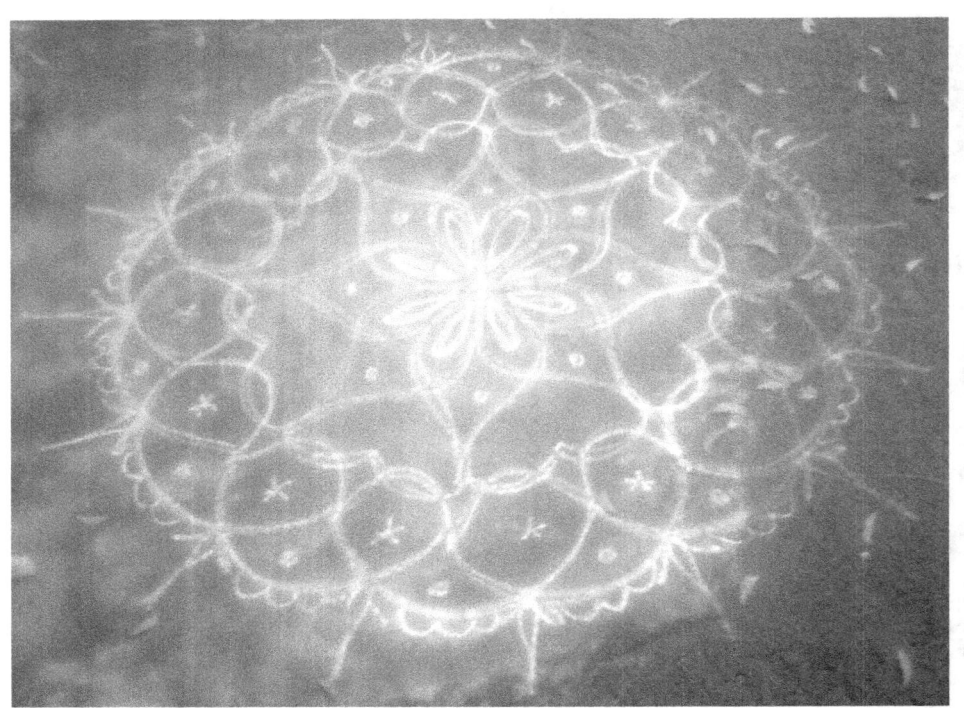

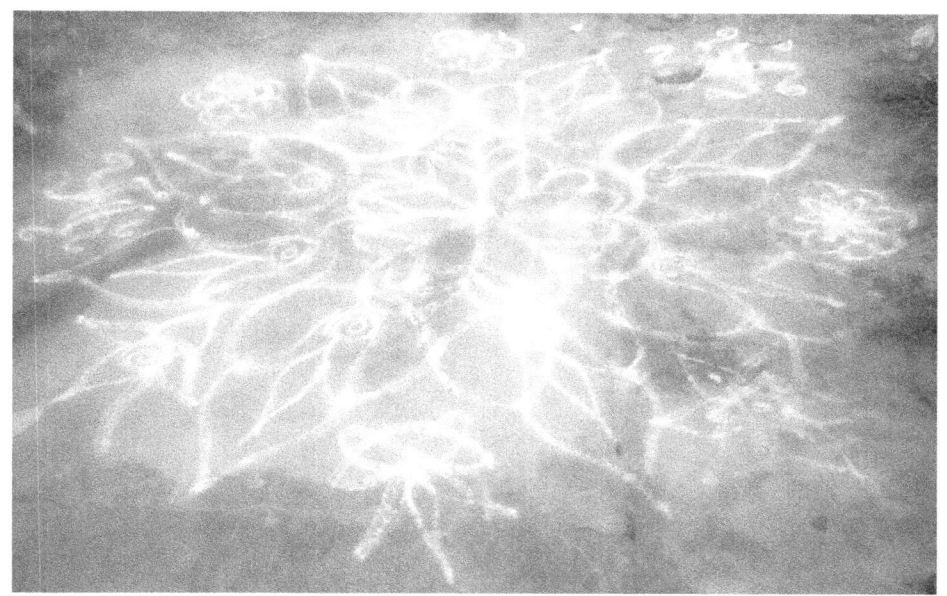

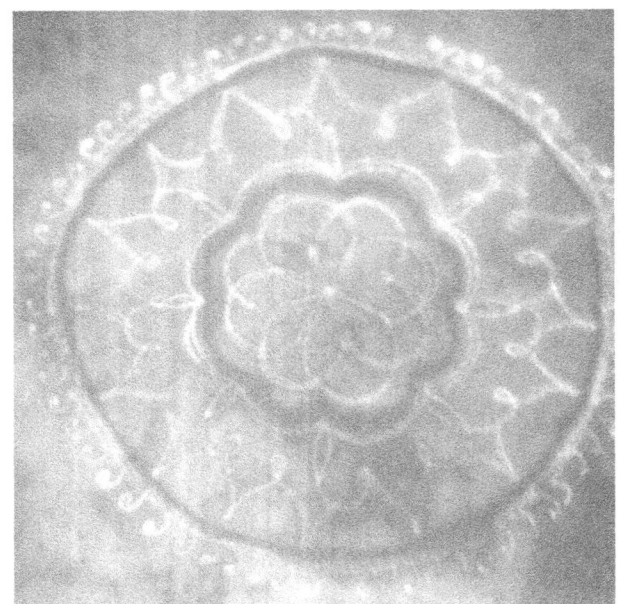

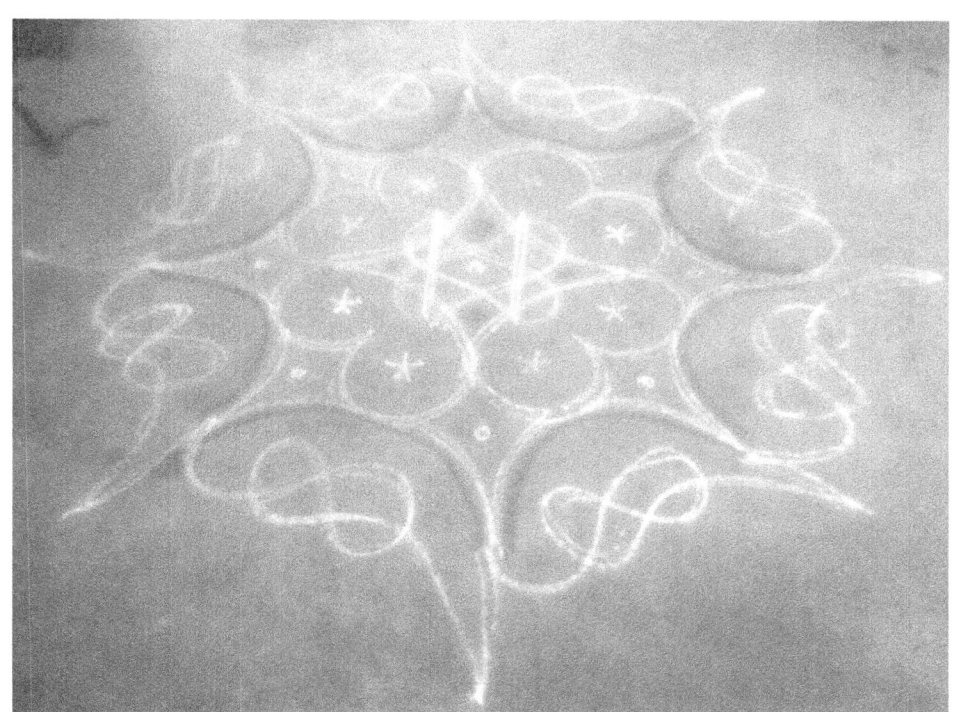

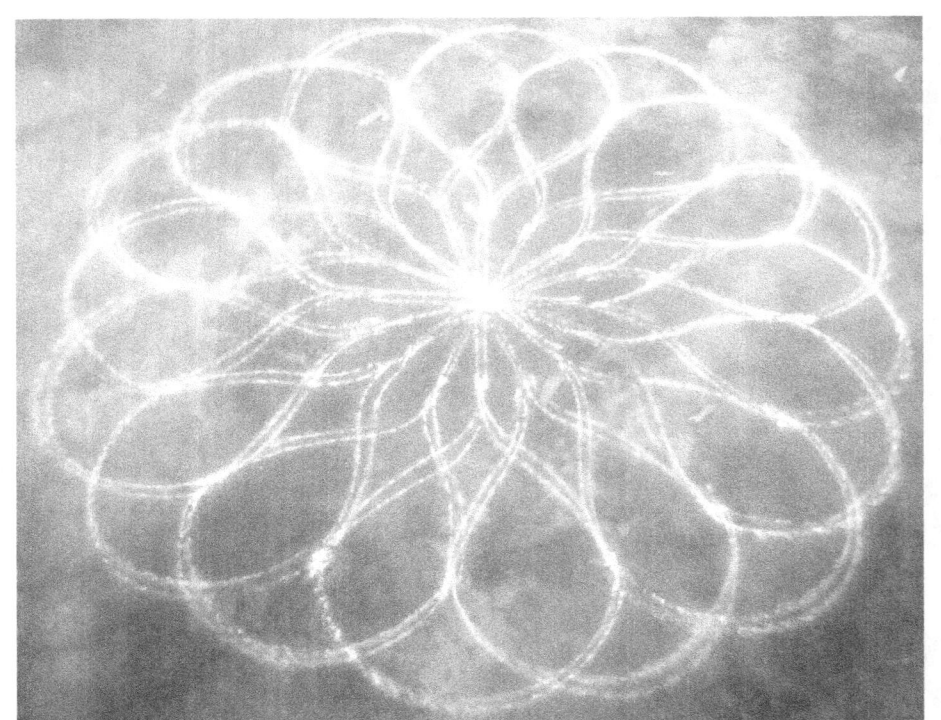